Does?

Do You Know What a

Book Publicist Does?

A Guide for Creating Your Own Campaigns

Claire McKinney

PLUM BAY PUBLISHING, LLC

Plum Bay Publishing, LLC
www.clairemckinneypr.com/plumbay

Library of Congress Control Number: 2017937772
ISBN: 978-0-9988617-0-8
Printed in the United States of America

Cover design by Lance Buckley
Interior layout by Barbara Aronica-Buck
Edited by Jeremy N. Townsend

First Edition

For Michael, Charlotte, and Veronica

Contents

SECTION I
The Basics

SECTION II
Preparing the Campaign

SECTION III
Reaching the Media

SECTION IV
Advanced Media Strategies

SECTION V
Events

SECTION VI
Last Words

SECTION I

•

The Basics

1.

Introduction

I decided to write this book several years ago, but I didn't know it at the time. It all started when *Publishers Weekly* published a piece I wrote in their "Soap Box" page in the June 27th, 2011, edition called "Do You Know What a Book Publicist Does?" I was inspired to write the Soapbox piece after a conversation I had with a colleague over lunch in Union Square a week or so prior.

Our discussion was about publishing houses, and how hard it was to get new ideas into the mix when it came to promotion and publicity. More specifically, we were talking about online media and how frustrating it was that there was a territorial battle taking place between marketing and publicity departments. This was making it terribly difficult for publicists to explore the vast world of print-to-online outlets, new websites, and bloggers—all of which could have been helpful in the promotion of books. In effect, I got worked up and ended up on my own soapbox, which led to writing the *PW* piece, and so on.

I received a lot of response to that piece, and I credit its journey across the Internet as one of the marketing tools that helped me start my own business. In addition to job leads, however, there were other more immediate comments such as: "It needed to be said," from a very prominent publicist and business owner, and "Do you think she'll get in trouble?" which was relayed to me by a colleague through a New York agent.

For years, journalists, especially at the trade publications, had been asking me to be a voice for publicists. I think they were really looking for juicy details about everything from screaming fits in departments to the reality of marketing in the publishing business. And the latter of the two comments above is the reason why neither I nor any of my other gainfully employed colleagues would say anything.

But what was there to say anyway? That bigger authors got bigger budgets? (I think anyone would know that). That we could tell stories of authors getting arrested, calling up to ask for an umbrella from 1,000 miles away, or receiving a phone call in the middle of the night from a writer on tour, in a bar, having a crisis? That a left-wing journalist refused to leave her hotel room without a blow-out every day? There are tons of these types of stories in any publicist's history, and although we have all managed situations good and bad, that is not what we do.

A publicist in any business that produces intellectual property, like publishing, film, and music, is responsible for promoting the idea or object that is produced along with managing the reputation of its creator. In my case, I have spent twenty years managing writers, academics, experts, and spokespeople while promoting their ideas, books, websites, and curricula. It's a great job that is ever-changing depending on the subject being discussed and there are many tools I use to communicate messages. The big-picture goal is to become a part of the larger conversation and to have a dialogue with others.

Press releases and pitches come from the publicist. We write and approve author bios, photos, branding on websites, talking points, and anything that will set the image for the person and set the stage for the idea or product being promoted. As an advanced communicator and public relations professional, I know that details matter, right down to the prepositions in a sentence. I also know that where and how you get the word out is a considerable part of whether your campaign will succeed.

Today, there are many types of media that exist under three major categories: traditional, digital, and social media.

- Traditional media: print, radio, and television;
- Digital media: websites, print-to-online, blogs, Internet radio, and video;
- Social media: Facebook, Twitter, Instagram, and LinkedIn, etc.

When you put together a media plan utilizing some or all of the outlets above, there are different factors that can affect what and when you pitch someone. Some of the questions I ask are: Do you have name recognition in your field? What and who are the primary competitors for your project? Is this your first time doing interviews? Are you comfortable on social media? Do you have a website? Is there breaking news in your story? Is your novel based on real events or people? The answers to these questions provide pieces of information that will help a publicist decide on a plan.

In this book, I am going to share with you the best way to

publicize books. Together we will delve into the elements of personal branding as it pertains to authors and experts who are selling ideas and/or books. For the most part, we will be looking at case studies of relatively unknown authors so you can see how to lay a solid foundation upon which to build future campaigns. I will explain what the primary media tools are and how best to reach and use them. I will also give you some advice on what to look for in a personal public relations person if you decide to hire someone to do the work for you.

I heard from a colleague recently who has left the book publicity business; she said she was glad to be in a new position where everything is not constantly changing. Allow me to give you some perspective: When I started working as a publicist, the Internet had been around for a while, but the first jobs featuring digital marketing descriptions were only just developing. For the most part, social media was about posting on message boards (and I made some message boards angry for promoting a book on fan sites).

Twenty years later, a publicist must take into account the cyber landscape as well as what she is able to book on the ground. There are unwritten rules and some published guidelines about how the Internet can benefit a book and author. I will share what I know with you in these chapters.

There are a number of publicists who have their own companies, as I do, or who freelance for authors. I am so disappointed when an author comes to me completely disillusioned because the publicist "didn't do anything," or didn't communicate well. I had been told by media people that it is hard to get a return response from a publicist these days. Really?! That is unbelievable, considering how hard it is to get a media contact's attention in this busy, newsy world.

Most of the publicists you meet are well-intentioned and have varying levels of experience. If you are reading this book, you will learn how to put together your own campaign, and in the process, you will learn what a publicist does so you can ask questions. Misunderstandings occur when expectations are not clear. If you are working with a person at a publishing house or someone you hire, you will be empowered to ask for what you want, and to find out what might not be possible. However, you are travelling on the journey to publicizing and promoting your book, and my goal is to help you achieve your goals. Let's get started!

2.

Publicity, Marketing, and Public Relations

When I was first introduced to publicity, I had no idea what it was. I had been working full-time as an assistant to the associate publisher/director of marketing for Hyperion Books for Children while at the same time pursuing a career in musical theater. My gracious boss had just let me take a six-week leave to do a regional show, and when I returned he and I had a heart-to-heart about my job description.

"John, I'm not sure what I'm doing with theater right now, but I know that the job you have me doing is boring. I need something more substantial to keep me engaged in the work," I said.

John looked up from his desk, leaned back in his chair and said, "Ok, why don't you do the publicity for the new imprint?"

The twenty-something me would have rather joined the Polar Bear Club than admit that I didn't know something, so I said, "Ok, sure." And that was that.

For the next couple of years, I learned the nuts and bolts of press releases, pitches, and media relations—who to call and who not to call. I became skilled at knowing how to talk about books and how to break down three hundred pages into a two-sided press release that would sell sand in the Mojave. I got a handle on how to communicate with bookstores and authors, create detailed schedules, book multiple city travel arrangements, and hire media escorts (the kind that drive authors to their media interviews). I made mistakes and had many successes. As it turned out, I was exceptionally good at the whole process. But after two years, even though I knew the method, I was missing many of the finer points of communications. Those came later with experience and a challenging environment where the media landscape seemed to be changing dramatically every year.

In the 1990s, everything was about the phone call. We had call sheets that listed the media outlets' names, numbers, and addresses, and I used to write notes along the side indicating what happened on each call. The print-out was from a dot matrix printer with these tear off strips with holes on the sides. We had an in-house database on the computer that you needed to speak to in DOS (no user-friendly Windows there).

Today, the first round of pitching usually happens by email, and some contacts prefer it that way. Calls are made, but not to everyone—like bloggers, who don't have their phone numbers listed. But the evolution of the tools of the trade and how we use them hasn't changed the essence of a publicist's job, which is about building relationships. We do this by creating messages that reach people and resonate with them. We communicate clearly and purposefully all the time. Strategies are developed intentionally to build momentum for a product, person, or idea. My point is, publicity and public relations have a skill set that can be taught, but they are also crafts that you work on as long as you are in the business. This is what keeps me interested and connected to the work, and it is where most of the misunderstandings between non-publicists and publicists begin to grow.

3.

The Building Blocks

We all know that we participate in a consumer-driven economy. Competition is fierce, and most people do not know what is entailed in reaching customers and developing the right kinds of relationships that will lead to long-term brand and sales success. The two major umbrellas that serve these purposes are **marketing** and **public relations**, and many things fall into these two camps.

According to the American Marketing Association, marketing is defined as: "The activity, set of institutions, and processes for creating, communicating, delivering, and exchanging offerings that have value for customers, clients, partners, and society at large."

In simpler terms, Yahoo says marketing is: "The strategic functions involved in identifying and appealing to particular groups of consumers, often including activities such as advertising, branding, pricing, and sales."

For people who are trying to sell a book, there are several ways to approach marketing. Let's break the definitions down and identify what each piece is intended to do:

"Appealing to particular groups" or Finding your audience: You need to answer some hard questions such as: Who is going to buy your book? Who is going to be interested in what you are saying? What are these people talking about now, and where can you find them?

"Branding": Decide what you and your book represent. How do you want to package yourself or what image do you want to project? What kind of packaging is appropriate? How can YOU appeal to your audience? Create language and visuals that go along with your choices.

"Advertising": When should you pay for exposure or audience reach? When the time is right, advertising is something to explore. The ad world has changed as much as the publicity world, and the subject is an entire volume onto itself.

Public Relations (PR), according to Yahoo, is "the art or science of establishing and promoting a favorable relationship with the public." I love the words "art or science" because they pertain to my earlier argument about the work ultimately being a craft based on a skill set and experiential knowledge. In layman's terms, PR is about getting the word out through appropriate messaging across many channels. First you create the story or message you want to broadcast and then, via traditional, digital, and social media, you propagate the information.

Messaging comes in many different forms, and for a publicist it can be press releases, original articles, podcasts, videos, and photos.

Knowing which of these is relevant to your topic and audience is part of your job when planning a publicity campaign.

Whereas a PR campaign might be driven by concepts and image along with product promotion, publicity is more focused on the completed product. In terms of books, this means that with all the preparation you have done in creating the book, the marketing package, the message, and image become important. Now it is all about getting to the right contacts, with the right message, at the right time, to get the coverage you want to further your goal, whether it be sales of a book, or growing your platform as an expert.

What is Your Book About?

FICTION

If someone asked you what your book is about, how would you answer? Can you respond in two or three sentences? Is it an interesting description that would make you stand up and pay attention? Clearly book topics and subjects will appeal to different types of people, and that is just fine. Knowing what you are delivering is a critical key in preparing a publicity campaign.

When you are determining what your book is and how you will describe it, you must envision the audience you are trying to engage with. If your book is a mystery, then say "It's mystery/thriller/suspense." Don't be shy about how you will explain it, either. Be completely confident and forthright in your response to the question. Then go on to mention the main character, the main points of action, the setting, and all those other things you used to answer on tests in high school literature classes. Remember *The Red Badge of Courage? Pride and Prejudice? Beowolf?* The way you shape your response to the question "What is your book about?" is the opportunity for you to hook a potential reader or media entity. Then you can dig deeper.

Do you remember learning about the latent and manifest themes in English classes? No. Well, I completely understand. If my kids weren't in school right now, I probably wouldn't think about these things either. But the manifest theme is similar to how you describe what your book is in two or three sentences. It's what you find on the surface: the main points, the selling points, and the overarching topic. The latent theme is a more in-depth look at what the book's themes are and what the author is trying to say. The latent components of your book are where there are more possibilities for marketing and publicity. In today's marketplace, being able to tap into the niche audiences beyond just book enthusiasts is when you get an edge over your competition. It may be the only way to make a significant dent in sales and get your voice heard.

Case Study:
The Organ Takers, by Richard van Anderson

The Organ Takers is a good example of many topics related to book publicity. For this example, let's look at our initial question: "What is your book about?"

At first glance, *The Organ Takers* is a medical suspense thriller. It's about a doctor with a family, and he becomes embroiled in an organ harvesting scheme that is run by another doctor who believes his scientific breakthroughs will save the world. Dead bodies and other collateral damage are all justified in the name of science and progress. Meanwhile, our doctor hero tries to do the mad scientist's bidding while hiding his illegal activities from the police, and protecting his family from murderous villains. The author intends that this be the first installment in a trilogy.

On the surface, the book has a clear path to be promoted in the mystery community, where there are many reviewers, bloggers, and

fans who can be reached through the Internet and at various traditional print outlets. But let's look at some of the layers we can use
to our advantage in the following chart.

Book Attribute	Author Attribute	Audience
• Suspense/Thriller • Medical Suspense • New York Setting	• Retired Cardiac Surgeon • Local Area • Medical expertise/ knowledge of organ harvesting legend	• Genre fans • Doctors with book blogs • Fans of Robin Cook and other similar writers • NYC book reviewers • Locally based media of all kinds • Fans of urban legends/conspiracy theorists

As you can see, there is much more to be explored in the name
of publicity and promotion, once you dig below the surface. As it
turns out, for Mr. van Anderson's book we were able to get him on
radio and television to talk about his background in relation to the
veracity of the tale in the book. The bottom line is that there is no
black-market organ harvesting going on in our area of the world.
And, medically speaking, it would be difficult to pull it off. So, we
know that our villain is just a fictional one, and everyone can rest
easy while holding onto their kidneys, hearts, livers, lungs, etc.

Another very cool aspect of Mr. van Anderson's book is that his
medical expertise and experience as an actual surgeon make the
descriptions of the operations very realistic. As a fan of the macabre
and inner workings of the human body, I found Mr. van Anderson's

expertise to be a terrific aspect of his story. As it turned out, there were other readers like me out there who found the same to be true and it made the enjoyment of the novel even better for them.

To get to the heart of your "story's story" and find the hidden chances for better publicity coverage, try answering the following questions:

1. What is your book about? (two to three sentences)
2. Where does it take place?
3. Where do you live?
4. Do you have any autobiographical contributions to the story, such as the medical expertise in our case study?
5. Who would find these aspects about you interesting?
6. Does your story address any "hot button" issues like civil rights, drug abuse, weight loss, relationships?

Once you have answered these and any other questions you might think of, fill in the table with potential audiences or media targets. You may be surprised at how much you can do, even with a work of fiction! In nonfiction, it is usually much easier to peel the onion, but being savvy about your subjects is still important.

NONFICTION

Nonfiction seems like it would be easy to dissect, but the large range of topics out there makes it tricky. The first step is to identify what kind of book you have written from your perspective. Is it prescriptive such as self-help or how-to? Is it a memoir? Is it historical, a cookbook, political? If you search for nonfiction subject areas you will find many of them, and sometimes the book you have written will fit into more than one area. You will need to determine which one(s) fits best when you start working on a promotion plan.

Case Study:
Why Him? Why Her?, by Helen Fisher

Why Him? Why Her? was written by Dr. Helen Fisher, who at the time was a consultant for Chemistry.com, a division of Match.com. The "manifest" content or subject for the book was clearly relationships, and *20/20* did a big special on the topic by focusing on dating couples and a singles night in a New York City club. The media schedule for this book was A-list all the way, but for Dr. Fisher there was much more to the story.

Why Him? Why Her? was not a simple, prescriptive self-help title focusing on dating. It was based on scientific research and evidence that showed people could identify their perfect matches by measuring hormone levels in the brain. Dr. Fisher is an anthropologist and a researcher who was fascinated with how people found each other and why love was such an important part of human existence. The possibilities for promotion have now grown beyond relationships.

If you apply the same exercise to Dr. Fisher's book that we did with our fiction example you will find the following:

Book Attribute	Author Attribute	Audience
• Finding your perfect match • Scientific basis	• PhD in Anthropology; international scientist • Academic • Author consults for Match.com	• Singles/dating couples • Science journalists/programs/academics • Universities and potential for course adoptions • Members of Match.com and its affiliates

The main difference between a novel and a nonfiction book like the one I have used here is that a novel will always be shelved as fiction. You will not be able to promote it as anything else, although you can use the author's expertise to find more publicity opportunities beyond book reviewers. For nonfiction, the book can have more than one category such as "relationships/science." From a bookseller's perspective, this labelling provides direction as to where to put the book in the store. Promotion combining the main subject of the book with any ancillary topics and the author's background can open up the book to a much bigger audience.

Who Are You?

In 2015, sources such as Bowker and Nielsen indicated that there were over 700,000 books published that year. Some of these were traditionally published, some were reissues, and many were self-published. No matter how the books came to market, that is a big number of titles circulating in the United States economy. In fact, it often seems like every other person you talk to is thinking about writing a book, or has one on the way. With the market being as crowded as it is, making you and your work stand out has never been more important. You will want to utilize *all* of the tools in your tool box and, like the previous chapter, use those that focus on the content of your book. Here I will delve deeper into what qualities make you a compelling and readable author.

Who are you? If you have ever tried to answer this question beyond just replying with your name, you know how difficult it can be. Are you a mother, wife, husband, father, teacher, gardener, doctor, cook, philanthropist, businessperson, mogul, CEO, or volunteer? Do you approach things philosophically? Are you super practical? Do you like to be in front of people? Do you prefer to be alone?

Responses to these questions combine to create an identity for an author that can be shaped and molded into the public persona you want to share with your audience. We all know the stories of reclusive, alcoholic, even mad writers. I even had a friend once who said he was going out to his buddy's empty beach house one winter to write the great American novel. A picture of my pal with an army blanket slung over his shoulders and a bottle of scotch clutched in one hand stuck with me until he returned, without a manuscript unfortunately. In today's world, the luxury of being that kind of private, eccentric writer is long gone.

With the many media venues and opportunities for people to engage with authors, it is now expected that you will meet your public in one way or another. Determining what aspects of "you" are going to be shared with the world comes from doing the kind of self-analysis inspired by the question "Who are you?"

What Are Your Goals?

There are many people writing books today who have agendas beyond just selling copies or being read in high school for years to come. Every celebrity is writing a memoir much sooner than one might think possible. What does Justin Bieber really have to contribute to the big picture of life on the planet to anyone over the age of twelve? Even politicians like Hillary Clinton planned publications based on campaign schedules for important positions like New York State senator and president of the United States. For us "regular" people there are career-focused reasons, or sometimes reasons that are benign.

Case Study:
The China Fallacy, by Donald Gross

For some people, writing a book is a natural evolution in their careers. Don Gross was a veteran of the State Department who left government work for a career as a consultant, specializing in the Pacific Rim. His book *The China Fallacy,* on U.S. foreign policy in the Pacific Rim region, was published by the academic division of Bloomsbury Publishing U.S.A. in 2013.

After a publicity campaign that included primarily radio and some television, Mr. Gross decided to continue promoting himself along with the book. When I worked with him, his goals were to increase his media platform and his exposure to the market discussing China, North and South Korea, and Japan. He wanted to find a couple of mainstream media outlets where he could be called upon to add his voice and opinion to the larger discussion about Pacific Rim policy and issues.

One of the first things I did was pitch and secure him as a regular blogger for *The Huffington Post*. He committed to writing a new post every two weeks that focused on some aspect of the news and his expertise. These posts were circulated to a long list of academics, colleagues, media professionals, and influencers. In Mr. Gross's case, the book opened the door to opportunities for him to speak to audiences, write more, and be interviewed as an expert on his subject. Eventually, by growing his public profile, he would be well-positioned to write another book and to even grow his consulting business.

Case Study:
Double Whammy, by Gretchen Archer

When Gretchen Archer first came to me she had recently published her first book, *Double Whammy*, a mystery featuring a peppy, colorful character named Davis Way. This book and her subsequent books are set on a riverboat casino in Mississippi called the Bellissimo. Gretchen is a smart, funny, Southern "housewife" (as she calls herself) whose kids are at a more independent age, thereby giving her more time to herself. Gretchen would probably say "not so much time," because she gets up at 3:00 or 4:00 a.m. to start writing.

Gretchen's goals are very much in line with the kinds of books she is writing. She wants to grow her career as a professional author, and she has been producing a series of books—one or two a year, depending on what she and her publisher have agreed to. To this end, promoting the Davis Way Crime Caper series is a long-term proposition, and one of my jobs as her publicist is to "build" Gretchen.

With any kind of series written by an unknown author, the publicity plan and promotional trajectory is about trying to get the most people to open the book and read it! Bloggers, book reviewers, trade reviews, author events, conferences, parties, local TV, radio, and print, are all pitched *all of the time*. The idea is to create a media list of fans who will support the books and the author by reviewing the books favorably and encouraging their readers to get the books for themselves.

Since Gretchen is building a business as an author, she sees the process like an entrepreneur, and gradually devotes more resources and time as the exposure and sales increase. Each book increases revenue exponentially because the first book is always promoted along with the current book, so readers can follow the life of Davis Way from the very first day she got into the private investigator business.

Each case above is about an individual building his/her career as an expert/writer or series novelist. As I've stated, your reason may be more benign at the start because you just need to write. If you don't know what your specific goals are, ruminate on the question and they will come to you, even if it is simply a desire to share a story. That in itself is admirable.

Why Did You Write Your Book?

Looking at who you are and what your goals are can answer the question of why, but I think it still needs to be addressed separately. Knowing the answer to "why" is the key to successfully presenting yourself and your work to achieve the best possible results. The answer to "why" is the "truth" or "integrity" attached to the work. It is the purpose, core, and foundation that will allow you to build whatever you want on it.

In order to answer the question, you need to be completely honest with yourself. If you hire a publicist, tell him or her, too. There is no bad answer, even if it's something along the lines of "I want to make a million dollars." Maybe you want to help people. Maybe you think you know something no one else does, and you need to educate people. Maybe the story in you is so pushy it just has to come out! Or, maybe you don't know, but you just wanted to get your thoughts and ideas down on paper.

The closer you can get to why and what your goals are, the clearer the path will be for promotion. Your reasons will inform how you approach your market, where you look for media attention, what you say to media professionals, and what you communicate in front of an audience. People can sense someone who is genuinely invested in what they have written. Giving your motivations a voice will make them more powerful; adding them to the topics and audiences that your book fits into will make the rest of the plan much easier to put together. Do these things first and you will be on the right path.

4.

Publicity in Self-Publishing vs. Traditional Publishing

To self-publish or traditionally publish, which should you choose? You may not have a choice. To traditionally publish you will need an agent. There are some publishers who will take unsolicited submissions if you know an editor or someone on the inside, but the majority will want agent entries only. If you don't have an "in" to the community of agents, finding one, sending a query letter and proposal, and waiting for a response can take years. If you get a positive response, you will have to come to terms with the agent and "get signed." Then the agent submits your work to publishing houses, which can take days or months depending on how marketable your manuscript is. The bottom line is: many now-famous authors went through this process and were rejected time and time again before finally getting somewhere.

J.K. Rowling and the Harry Potter series is one of the ultimate examples of someone who submitted to a slew of publishers and was finally accepted by Bloomsbury UK. She has been very upfront about the journey and how hard it was. Yet her story is still an anomaly.

The majority of writers looking for agents are rejected at the first line of defense. I can't tell you how many authors I've talked to who have broken this barrier, gotten an agent, and were then turned down by editors and publishing houses for a variety of reasons. Some of the responses writers have received say the writing is good, but the book is going to have a hard time finding an audience; they just aren't accepting many new novelists (memoirists, etc.) at this time; or there are too many books on the subject and the timing isn't right. All of these come down to not having an adequate enough market for a publisher to justify signing up the book on a P&L statement.

For our purposes, let's say you are being traditionally published and you have the marketing and publicity muscle of professionals at your beck and call. Think again. Just because you have a signed contract and a brand on the spine does not mean you will get everything you are looking for in a publicist.

"In-house" publicists often have more than one book to promote every month, and there are always judgment calls to be made. Sometimes your boss tells you what your priorities are, and sometimes you have to make the decisions. Think of it this way:

A publicist has twelve books to work on in a six-month season. Six of them are novels. There is one *New York Times*, *LA Times*, *Fresh Air*, insert your own media outlet, etc. Realistically how many of the novels will get the brass ring of review coverage in mainstream outlets? Answer: One, none, a couple here and there?

Oftentimes it's a numbers game when you are dealing with that many books, and I know that in many of the big houses the lists these people manage could be even larger than this example.

Margins in Publishing

By the way, the margins in publishing in general are rarely good because it is very, very difficult to predict the sales outcome, even with decades of experience. Publishers often lose more money than they make, especially when they take on unknown authors without already significant marketing platforms. This accounts for some of the success of celebrity bios. Snooki sells, and so does Hillary Clinton, Rob Lowe, and many other familiar names you will find on the nonfiction side of bestsellers lists.

Here's one way to think about it: The general rule when I worked in house was that a marketing budget was seven percent of the amount of the author's advance. Now you can do the math to figure out what the likely percentage of effort, money, and time will be spent on your book versus others that the company has to produce.

From a marketing and publicity perspective, the advantages to traditional publishing are not what you might have fantasized about. No matter what, you will need to know how publicity works and what you need to ask so you have a clearer idea of the kind of support you will get from the publisher, and what you will need to contribute either on your own or by hiring a professional.

Self-Publishing

When you think about it, self-publishing has been around for centuries because there were no big publishing houses when the first words and phrases were immortalized on paper. Someone had to start the process, and the only way to determine whether a book was good was if someone, or a lot of people, read it.

Today, the story is similar in that many people who have heretofore not been able to get published have venues and opportunities to do it themselves. When I first started working on my own in 2009, the self-publishing movement was just gathering steam and the quality of books was very different from what I see today. That makes sense, because many people were flying blind and had to clear the path so that future writers would be able to follow a process and know where to find editors, book designers, publicists, printers, and everything else.

For the self- or indie-published authors, it has not been easy to publicize or market their work. There are many different reasons, but most prevalent is that without a publishing professional to tell you how the industry works, you don't know what the rules are with bookstores, events, and media outlets, and you don't have the contacts to connect to for help.

The other issue is that while you were nurturing your book and watching the buzz surrounding other titles in the market, you didn't know that you were not going to have the same opportunities. The bottom line is that book reviews in traditional outlets like the *New York Times* or *USA Today* are not available for the indie author. In fact, trade reviews in *Booklist, Library Journal, Publishers Weekly,* and *Kirkus* are not available unless, if the publication offers an indie review service, you pay a fee.

There has been a "stigma" against the self-published, and there is some history behind it. Traditionally published writers may feel that you must pay your dues before you get to have a book in the marketplace. They did it, and therefore you have to as well. I've been there: in a past life I was an actor in New York, and just as I was about to become eligible to get my card and get into equity auditions on Broadway, the Actor's Equity Association cut the eligibility program. Word on the bitter side of the street was that the unionized actors didn't want to share.

In addition to being cut out of certain media outlets, indie authors have to work harder at getting events at book stores because they don't have wide distribution, a topic we will get to later. Most of the chain booksellers like Barnes & Noble won't host you for an event unless you have a relationship with the store. Even then, some stores only book their events through their corporate offices, which won't entertain a self-published title. Independent bookstores may host an author, but they may charge a fee and the books will be sold on consignment, so you will have to ship them or bring them to the store yourself and take the process from there. You may also have to convince the store that you will be able to bring in an audience. When I started working with self-published authors, I didn't realize the extent of the differences when it came to publicity and promotion. I've learned a lot and have been successfully helping people who have hired me, but I am not immune to learning something new.

Indie Stores vs. CreateSpace

Recently I took on a client who had a wonderful relationship with a bookstore in her town, which happened to be a very book-oriented community. She had been buying her books in the store for fifteen years and was finally publishing her own book that, though fictional, was tied to a news story that had happened in the area. We all thought it would be a simple matter to book an event for her with the store.

We called the store and got the information for the events coordinator who worked off-site, and we contacted her explaining that our client was a local author. To our tremendous surprise we got denied. And not just a simple "no thank you, this isn't right for us" or "we are too booked right now"—we got an admonishment from this person accusing us of not representing reputable authors. Shocking!

A few weeks of back and forth ensued before we got our client involved, because she had a right to know that the store she had been loyal to for years was so opposed to hosting her. And not only that, we had booked a piece on the book in the local online paper, and everyone was asking if her book would be available at the local store. "Sorry," we all said, "you'll have to go to Amazon or Barnes & Noble."

After a few weeks, we found out that this independent bookstore, and others around the country, have been boycotting any authors who have published their work with CreateSpace, an Amazon self-publishing vehicle. This reasoning was tied to another policy held by the majority of indie stores to not stock or sell any books published by Amazon Publishing, which has a few traditional imprints under its umbrella.

To us, this is a strange way to connect the dots, because Amazon as a publisher is unrelated to CreateSpace. One is a corporate publishing endeavor (Amazon Publishing), the other is a service purchased by individuals who don't have the means to print a book on their own (CreateSpace). Needless to say, the author was quite upset by all of this, and though the store did offer an option for her to appear at a local author event, they were very clear that they would not publicly support or promote her visit. We would have done that work anyway as her publicists—but the store would not do anything, including put her book in the window, make a sign, or stock/order the book for customers who knew her and also wanted to support their local bookstore.

As I said, there are still things to learn in the frontier that is self-publishing, but you will find in the pages of this book that there are many clear ways to spread the word, get media attention, and make public appearances.

More on Richard van Anderson

Remember Richard van Anderson from our discussion of marketing and publicity angles in your book? His is also a good example of how a campaign for a self-published book can work.

Richard is serious about his writing career. Not only was he a cardio-thoracic surgeon, but when he left that career he earned an MFA in creative writing. He figured out what he wanted to write, established a website, got an editor, hired a jacket designer, started a social media presence, set up his own publishing imprint and logo, and published a short story ahead of the book to introduce himself to a reading audience. Then he hired us.

We worked on getting reviews for the book, local media, bookstore events in his area, and pitching him for a regional crime writing conference. He agreed to pay for a listing in *Publishers Weekly*, which also considered his book for review.

Using the tools I mentioned earlier, we were able to get review coverage from bloggers and websites that reviewed fiction, crime fiction, and medical thrillers. We even found a small community of doctors who had written books in the same category as Richard's and wanted to review it. *Publishers Weekly* loved the book, gave it a starred review, and named him one of their self-publishing stars of the year. He was featured in the magazine three separate times.

Van Anderson was profiled and interviewed in his local glossy magazine and had an event for all of his associates, friends, and neighbors. We took the nonfiction related angles of the book and got him radio interviews. When he went to the crime conference, a local morning program on the top television network in the market interviewed him.

We took all of these things and presented them to the primary discount e-book distributor BookBub, which after three submissions, finally scheduled the book for a promotion. Seven months after the book came out, he told me he had just exceeded sales of 6,000 print/digital copies. Not too shabby for a first-time writer doing it on his own.

Traditional Publishing

If you are traditionally published, there are different levels of publicity support based on the budget assigned to your book. When I was working in house, the base level was a review campaign, which would include a press release and mailing to all of the major book review outlets, including trades. In the publisher's catalog your campaign would say "National Review Campaign" to represent the publicity support. There would likely be a couple of other lines indicating other marketing functions.

A top level campaign would look something like this:

- National Review Campaign
- National Broadcast Campaign
- National Print Features/Interviews
- National 10–20-city Author Tour
- Blog Review Campaign
- TV/Radio Satellite Tour

The budget for the above is at least $50,000 with some fluctuation, depending on the tour markets, travel costs, and whether a satellite tour is booked on radio or TV, etc. A publicist managing this campaign should have virtually nothing else to do that month except maybe a review campaign, and the level of publicist assigned to the book would be at least a senior.

A small or low-level campaign would look something like this:

- National Review Campaign
- Blog Review Campaign

The campaigns in between these two extremes vary by book and budget. If you choose to rely exclusively on the publicist assigned to you by the publisher, here are some of the questions you need to ask to make sure you know what you will be receiving.

- Who is my publicist and when can I speak to him/her?
- How many review copies will the publicist have and when will they be ready?
- When will my campaign begin and when will I need to be available for interviews or events?
- When will I get a draft of the press release?
- Do you need me to provide a list of potential media contacts or suggest different audiences that may be interested in the book?
- Will you be organizing events at bookstores or libraries? What do you need from me in order to do this?
- Will you be pitching online reviewers?
- What kind of coverage do you think I can get?
- Is there anything that I should do on my own that would supplement the publicist's efforts?

I recommend you present these questions to your agent, editor, and anyone else you have access to at the publishing house when you enter into an agreement.

Most of the time the publisher is going to stress the editorial process and getting the book finished will be the priority. In my experience, by the time the publicist picks up the ball, the author has very little information about how to market a book. It would be helpful for everyone if the process was clearer so that there is time for you, the author, to do some of your own groundwork, hire a publicist, or enlist friends and family to start exploring what you will need to do in order to give your work the best chance of reaching the largest audience.

SECTION II

•

Preparing the Campaign

Now that you have identified various target markets for your book and understand some of the principles regarding how a traditional or indie book campaign is set up, it's time to start developing your own plan.

Because of the Internet, publicity campaigns today have a much greater reach than those we used to run when I started twenty years ago. Whereas a typical plan would consist of events and media (print, radio, and TV), now there are other tools to consider, such as social media, content marketing, and online media outlets (print-online, blogs, video, Internet radio). I used to tell people that the Internet was going to be like another media dimension with the same forms but on an elevated "plane," a.k.a. cyberspace. They would look like the ones on the "ground," but be seen elsewhere. I was never certain people understood what I was talking about, or if they thought I was just delusional, but today I see that everything I imagined is now real, and it's a lot of ground to cover for any publicist.

We are going to focus on the basic tools and organization of media and events, saving social media and content disbursement for another time. On the resources page, you will find a link to a free download of Social Media 101, *a basic guide to the major platforms that can help you with networks like Facebook and Twitter, if you aren't already chatting it up with the virtual community.*

5.

The Press Kit

To get started, you will need to refer to your answers on what the book is about and the different subjects it may cover. You will also incorporate why you wrote the book and figure out all of the people you know who could help you with the promoting process. These things will be blended into your main tool, the press kit. They are:

1. Press release
2. Your bio
3. Author Photo
4. Q&A
5. Talking Points
6. Praise sheet (if you've been reviewed already)
7. List of everyone you know well enough to engage with
8. List of towns/cities where you believe at least twenty people would come out to see you talk about your book
9. List of organizations or institutions that might be interested in your topic(s)

Creating a Press Release

There has been debate about press releases and whether or not they are obsolete. After all, when you can communicate in 140 characters, why do you need four to five paragraphs? I have heard directly from book review editors that they toss the materials that come with review copies. I have also had a radio producer chastise me for mistakenly not sending a press packet with a book. Clients have asked me if press releases matter anymore: "I mean, does anybody really read those things?" The short answer is "yes": there are media, booksellers, librarians, academics, etc., who do pay attention to an old-fashioned press release, and you have no way of knowing who is going to insist on having one and who isn't. So, I wouldn't throw out this tool just yet. Below are the main reasons why you should write and include a release with your kit.

1. **The Core Message**: Press releases are different from any of the other copy you will use to market your book. Some of the words may be the same as what you have on the back of the jacket, but the release is supposed to achieve a few things, including delivering the newsworthy or unique aspects of what you are presenting; giving the reader an idea of why you would be a good interview subject; and a relatively brief synopsis of the best points of the book (or product, depending on your industry).

2. **Press Approved Copy, or When Your Words Come Back to Haunt You**: This is my favorite. First of all, the copy on your release is assumed to be vetted and usable for the press. It is likely that one outlet or another will just lift the synopsis, or even the entire release, and reprint it online or in the newspaper. The first time I saw this it was a little weird, but by the very nature of what the document is, the words on the release are fair game for repurposing.

3. **SEO Optimization**: Having the release available on your website, your publicist's, publisher's, etc., gives you more real estate online and can offer more search results. You will notice a search for your book brings up Amazon.com and other big properties first; your publisher and your own website can appear on the first or near the top of the second page. It gives you more power online when there are more references to you and your work.

4. **The Pitch Package**: So many people interact primarily on email these days, so there is a bit more "room" to present the best aspects of your book. As a standard practice, we write pitches to fit the people to whom we are sending them, and we paste the press release below so the media contact can choose to learn more about the book. In the past, we would send a cover letter with the press kit, which constituted the pitch, and I know that today all of those pages won't get read in a mailing. The release is an informational supplement that provides another tool for marketing. If a contact only wants

to read three sentences, fine. If more is desired, it's all there in the email.

5. **Standard Practices**: More people want to see a release than not because it's part of the public relations/media relations process. In addition, your booksellers, event coordinators at higher-end venues, and librarians want to see the meat of what you are selling without having to read the entire book. Having a press release gives you a more serious, professional persona when you are marketing your book. It says you mean business and people should pay attention to you. Don't sell yourself short.

The other more esoteric reason for the release is that it is an opportunity for you and your publicist to come to an understanding of what your intention is about your book and its relevance. You may also discover some things that are unclear about your work, or an interpretation that is not at all what you meant. It's important to be fully aware of how the book will be presented and to settle on the message that you would feel comfortable with if it ran in a newspaper or online.

The structure of a release is based on how much interesting or provocative information you can share without overhyping your message. When you introduce the book, in the opening paragraphs, you will need to identify it using the entire title with the subtitle and in parentheses include the publication date, imprint, format, price, and ISBN like this:

The Great Book: A Novel by Bobbie Bobs (Imprint Name, Publication Date, Format, ISBN, Price).

The first one or two paragraphs should tell the reader of the release why this is a compelling book and what its relevance is to the audience. You will also want to explain why you wrote the book and how your story personal story is connected to it.

The following paragraphs should be a short synopsis of the plot if you are promoting a novel, and a list of the main facts or talking points if you are working on nonfiction. You can also include a more in-depth section on yourself and your story as it relates to the content if you have a strong personal connection to the material.

Within the release, you will want to mention the book's title at least three times. In the final paragraph, you need to develop an action statement that will tie up everything you have said so far and will encourage the reader to pick up the book and open it! Before you hit spell check, add your short bio under "About the Author": and the specs of the book (the ISBN, etc.) below that. Finish it off with the traditional "# # #" centered on the bottom, which indicates to the media person that all of the words preceding the symbols are approved for the press. To read some examples of releases, go to my website www.clairemckinneypr.com and click on the jackets under "Current" or "Previous Campaigns."

Writing a Good Bio

When I was young and naïve, I thought the bios you read in theater programs and on the backs of books were written by someone who had a lot of nice things to say about the person. In other words, I didn't know that individual people wrote their own. From that perspective, I started to categorize them by how much ego the subject had in order to write such glowing praise about himself! I was amazed at how much people touted their own accomplishments. I don't know about you, but I find it difficult to write about myself. I feel much more comfortable singing the praises of other people. However, in order to sell our books, we all need to try to channel that egomaniac and compose a good bio. There are two forms to consider. One is a brief, three-to-four sentence paragraph that can go on the back jacket of your book. The other is a lengthier explanation that could be found on a separate page in your book under "About the Author" or as a separate page in your press kit, along with your author photo. To help you get started, try answering some questions:

1. Where did you go to college and what degrees do you have? If you attended an MFA program or writer's retreat, where?
2. Where do you live? How many children/pets do you have?
3. What do you do during the day? (I.e., what's your day job? Are you a full-time caregiver?)
4. Do you have any previously published articles or books? What are they?

5. Are you a member of any organizations or do you serve on the boards of any non-profits? What are they?
6. What are your special interests?
7. Have you been interviewed, reviewed in, or written for any media outlets? What were they?
8. What is your website address, Facebook, Twitter, Instagram, Tumblr, LinkedIn handles?

Now take a look at everything you have noted above, and highlight all of the information you would want to read about someone with a book like yours. What gives you credibility? What makes you interesting as a writer? People these days are accustomed to looking into private lives on the Internet, and they feel entitled to know about their authors. This holds true even more if you have written a work of nonfiction. Then your education and other items that relate to your credibility become super important. Once you have pulled out all of the material that could go into your bio, you are ready to write. If you haven't already looked at author bios in the books you have on your shelves, do so. You can model yours after theirs to fit the style and length that you need. The short bio should list your credentials and education, especially for nonfiction; your affiliations; and perhaps the state and/or city in which you live. You are not required to print your address for all the world to see, but telling people the region where you reside is a nice way to give readers some perspective on what your lifestyle might be. You can mention your kids and pets as well, but it isn't a requirement. Again, these are just additional personal details that bring potential book buyers closer to you as a person/writer.

For the longer bio you should write about three paragraphs that fit on approximately three-quarters of a page. In this version, you will have more freedom to talk a bit more about why you wrote the book, what your interests are, etc. Just take a look at the questions you answered earlier to find the material with which you have to work. Any bio is an opportunity for an author to come out of the book to say "hi" to a reader. Make it your own. In this longer version, it is easier to be you.

If you have a sense of humor, let it come through. If you are more straight-laced and like to stick with the facts, then do that. Most of all, do not be afraid to talk about the good things you have done. After you have written your long and short form bios, have a friend, family member, colleague, or a neighbor take a look and provide some feedback. I like to have several sets of eyeballs check out anything I write and always accept feedback (even if I grit my teeth during the delivery of it). Get it done and check it off your list.

Your Photo

Many years ago, I was sitting at a dinner I had organized at Bouchercon, a consumer mystery convention. The guests included booksellers, authors, agents, and the publisher of Little, Brown. During dinner, we had an interesting conversation about "author photos" and whether or not they were necessary or important, and whether or not they needed to be in color or if it was okay to continue to use black and white. I bet even thinking that we would not have color photos in today's online visual world is amusing, so let me put it in perspective.

At that time "Friendster" was the big social media platform. There was no Facebook, and MySpace might have been creeping up on the horizon. Twitter, Instagram, Snapchat, Pinterest, YouTube, or Google+ didn't exist. The extent of online book reviews were sites like Bookloons, and barnesandnoble.com had an active editorial site connected to its fledgling online bookstore. In our twenty-first-century world, color photos are an absolute must. Plus, you need to have a cadre of other images that help illustrate your message or product. Back then color was just emerging, but in my opinion it was a simple way of adding an asset to the press kit that could be the difference between getting into a magazine or newspaper or not. But as has been my experience in this business, I was the upstart in the group.

Back at dinner, the conversation got rather lively regarding the relevance of author photos. "Does anyone really care what an author looks like?" asked the agent. Some people at the table, not wanting to contradict a potentially higher ranking member of the industry, said little. The publisher, my boss, asked, "Hmmm, Claire, what do you think from a publicity standpoint?"

Invited to speak my mind, I was quick to say, "It absolutely matters, and readers do care what the author looks like. And beyond that, magazines prefer to run photos in color, so we should really consider asking our authors to have color photos taken."

"Really?" the agent asked. "I find it hard to believe it truly matters."

"Well," I replied, "consider some of the popular authors like Sebastian Junger. Look at his photo and tell me it isn't important. Or pay attention to which authors end up with their photos included as part of a magazine or newspaper review. In a visual medium, the picture is going to have an impact."

You don't need to look like a model or a movie star to have a decent photo, but spending the time to get a decent picture will make a difference. Not too long after that evening, color images became the norm around the industry, but there were holdouts for a long time. Color was more expensive to produce, and we didn't have as many options for emailing images as we do today. It was likely that a hard copy of the photo would go into the press kit, and the same photo would be printed on the jacket. The bottom line is, it is important to make the best possible first impression with the media, and your photo is one of the tools you have (in addition to a bio and press release) to do that.

Do you have to spend a fortune on a professional photo shoot? Not necessarily, but you should do the best you can to secure the finest image. First, look at other author pictures on books and websites. See what "look" you like. Decide whether you want something inside against a plain or basic background, or if you want to be outdoors, in natural light. Do you have any current photos that could be good? Who is going to take the picture? Will you use a professional photographer or is your spouse handy with a camera or phone? Here is a checklist that can help you prepare:

- **Image/Wardrobe:** You need to have a couple of different outfits on hand so you can compare after you have taken your photos. Are you writing about secret agents and spies? A sharp suit is probably most appropriate. Are you a chef? Aprons, hats, and other kitchen accessories would be useful for your wardrobe. For women: do you wear makeup? Either go to your local mall's makeup counter to get a professional's touch for the day of the photo shoot, or hire a makeup or salon technician for a couple of hours. For men: you don't need to worry as much about the makeup, but getting a fresh haircut or considering whether you want that Michael Mooreish baseball hat as a prop is your homework for your shoot.

- **Scope of picture:** In the performing arts, agents and directors expect what they call "three-quarter shots," which typically include your face, upper body, and maybe your legs. You can decide what you want to do, and even if you do a full body picture, you can crop it to meet your needs. Whatever you do, don't let anyone twist you into a pretzel or convince you that you look better with your hand on your face. Just look at the camera and try to be as relaxed as possible, unless there is a connection to your work that requires something unorthodox.

If you are writing a treatise on how to bungee jump and want to be seen hanging from a bridge, please by all means do it.

- **Location:** Whether you decide on indoors or outdoors, make sure the background of the shot is clean of debris or unnecessary items that will take the focus away from you. That shiny, peacock print wallpaper might look great around the mantle, but will cause the viewer of the image to peer at your photo and desperately try to figure out what she is seeing. Garbage cans, giant leaf bags or garden tools, a sink full of dishes, etc., are all "better" viewed off camera.

- **Photo specs:** Your final photo needs to be at least 300 dpi and can be stored as a jpeg, tiff, or gif file on your computer. A downloadable picture should live on your website under your "media kit" or "press" tab. Your image should also be found on your book, bio, and any other marketing materials or social media accounts you use.

Why a Q&A?

After you have your press release, photo, and bio squared away, it's time to round out your press kit with information that can help you get interviewed, book events, and discover great pitching material. I recommend doing a Q&A for both fiction and nonfiction books.

A Q&A is composed of about six or seven questions with answers that can fit on two sides of a single page. Anything longer is too much and likely won't be read by a media person. The questions should relate to you as a writer or expert, any news that might be in the book, characters and themes, and other insights that only you can impart as the author of the book.

In general, Q&As can help you or a publicist hone in on angles that will help promote the book. They can also be sent to producers as sample interview questions; bookstores and event venues, so they can get a better idea of what you and your work are about; and they may be posted on blogs or websites that you pitch for promotion of the book.

Talking Points

Talking points are primarily used to get producers and hosts interested in interviewing you. Nonfiction topics are easier to break down on their own or by connecting to current events. However, novelists can also be promoted with their expertise in a subject area that may have led to the writing of the book.

For example, one of our clients is a PhD in Psychology and has been a family therapist for over twenty years. She wrote a young adult novel about a specific issue that occurred in high school between a girl and her teacher. There is behavioral science information about this problem that is relevant to her credentials and expertise. In addition, the book was inspired by an event that took place in her town, so from a local perspective this was very interesting.

Most of all, putting together Q&As and talking points is not meant to be stressful. There is no wrong answer here because only you know the answers to the questions, and you are in the best position to pull notable facts together that could interest media. I've had to answer questions like "What are these for?" "Who sees them?" and even, "Why do you need them?" I've had clients delay writing their answers to the point where we couldn't use them, which I believe was out of fear of portraying the wrong image or message. My answer is: you have to be willing to say something, make a point, or reveal an insight that will bring people closer to you and your book. This is the only way you will be able to connect with people and convince them that you have something to say that is different from the author who was knocking at their doors yesterday.

Praise Sheets

A praise sheet is an add-on to the press kit. If you don't have one, don't worry about it. This item is most commonly developed by authors who have been reviewed already for a previous work and/or who have received advance reviews for the current book.

The sheet will have a title, such as "Praise for BOOK by Jimmy Johns," or "Praise for the works of Jimmy Johns." Below that will be a list of endorsements or quotes attributed appropriately. The easiest way to give you advice on how to set this up is by listing some guidelines:

1. Do list the quotes in order of importance. Bigger media outlets first, best quotes first, most recognizable name first, etc. If your book received a great quote from *Publishers Weekly,* it should be listed first. You can also use praise from bloggers, especially if the blog is popular and well known.
2. Don't list quotes that are five or six sentences long. If a person sends you an endorsement that is this extensive, edit it a bit and send it back asking for permission to use it in truncated form for the press kit.
3. Don't list quotes attributed to "reader." This happens most with newer authors who try to entice press by showing them how many people like the book. In a pitch, you could mention you have "over one hundred 5-star reviews on Amazon" or something like that.
4. Don't add quotes that are by people who have absolutely no connection to the work. The point of the sheet is to show

how credible you and your work is, right? If you have a quote from the ring leader of Barnum and Bailey Circus for a book on foreign policy, it's disconcerting to someone who knows what's what. For example, Merle Bombardieri, therapist and author of *The Baby Decision*, has a praise sheet that lists quotes from other therapists and colleagues.

5. Do limit your attributions to one line. I've seen quotes from the attributed person listed along with his three previously published books. That is a great way for his work to get some promotion, but this is for you and you don't need to dedicate the real estate on the page to an attribution that takes up two lines. Of course, you should let your contact know that you need to shorten the identifier a bit and you can ask, "Which of these titles do you need me to list?"

The main thing to remember is that trying to create praise or embellish the credentials of someone who has written about your book on Amazon is seen for what it is. You will have nice things said about you by media, experts, and other authors. When you do, slap those quotes down on paper.

6.

Who Do You Know and How Can They Help You?

Are you the kind of person who asks for help? Or do you buckle down, grin and bear it, try to make it on your own, imagining you are an army of one? Do you hate having to ask? Why can't people just *know* that you need something? We all know that just isn't possible. So, if you are great at reaching out, then this won't seem so bad, but if you are the more stoic, "I can do it on my own" type, this next step isn't going to be easy. You can't do this on your own so you will have to get over yourself and start building your army of helpers and word-of-mouth.

Everyone talks about word-of-mouth and how to make it spread. It may look like a big media hit caused the snowball effect that led to the success of someone's book, but I promise you that wasn't the beginning of the story. In fact, I can tell you in the case of a hugely successful novel, *The Lovely Bones*, that it took an entire publishing house to build the buzz that started the runaway train to make that book a tremendous bestseller.

I was at Little, Brown at the time and at every meeting with someone from the outside, or to get people interested within the company, the book was always a topic of conversation. The effort got people to read it, and because it *was* a good book, momentum started to grow. And that's the thing about promoting your book—you need people to open the cover and start reading. Is there a magic spell? No. It starts with everyone you know.

This is what you are going to do. Sit down with a notebook and a pen or at your computer, whatever works for you. Now in one column make a list of all the people you know. They can be family, friends, coworkers, chatty local store owners, and people whose business cards you have. Former teachers, the parents of your kid's friends, people on Facebook with whom you have interacted, and people on other social media networks. Take a look at your list—this is where you will start your campaign.

Make a second column that indicates how well you know the person and make a note next to each name. Then put their contact information including email and address (if you have it). Now create a column called "What do I want/need?" This is where you will decide how this contact can help you. Here is a sample to get you started:

Name	Nature of Relationship	Contact Info	How can they help?
Jill Smith	Best friend	jill@yahoo.com	Amazon review
Ben Jones	Works at HuffPo	ben@huffpo.com	Review connection

Your goal with most of the people on your list is to make them aware of the book. You may want to gift copies to some of them so they may read them and post reviews on Amazon and/or Goodreads. It's possible once you start reaching out to your list that you may only have a couple of degrees of separation from a media contact who could help you get the book reviewed, or get you booked on a radio or television program. I can bet you that you actually know more people than you think you do.

Now comes the hard part: It's time to figure out how to "ask." First, make an announcement on Facebook and other social media platforms you use regularly so those people know about your book. Then take out your colored highlighters and indicate who on the list you know well, who is a business connection, who is a friend of a friend, who you know from social media, and any other relationships that apply. For individuals on the list you know well, you can write a personal note and send a copy of the new book. In the note, I would write: "When you've had a chance to read my book, if you would post a review on Amazon.com, that would be great!" Then when someone does respond or does what you ask, make sure to send that person a thank you note.

If you aren't directly connected to a person, you can send an email asking if he or she would like to receive a copy of your book and/or, if you have a publicist working for you, ask the contact if it would be okay for your publicist to contact him directly. If a close friend or relative of yours is in touch with someone you want to reach, ask if an introduction could be made that would allow you to communicate directly with that person. While you are at it, make a wish list of all of the prime influencers you would climb mountains to reach and see if anyone in your personal network has a way to get to them. You never know. It's a six-degrees-of-Kevin-Bacon world, and you might even be able to get to him—if that would help.

What I want you to take away from this section is that you have your own army already under your influence. You just need to assemble them and direct them to what you need done. People want to help if they can. Sometimes a person is too busy to respond right away, or may never be able to make a direct impact, but just putting your news and requests out into the world can yield results. There will be some surprises, and at times it will seem like nothing is happening, but there will be things in the universe that will happen in spite of you and without your knowledge.

7.

What is a Pitch and How to Write One?

This is a topic that will be covered substantially in the next section when you finally get to work on the media effort for your campaign. For now, I want to explain what a pitch is and what the main components are of a good one. I have found that authors are much more comfortable summarizing their books than they are "selling" them. A pitch needs to sell something, plain and simple. Did you know you were getting a job in inside sales? I think not, but let's call it what it is, get over any squeamishness, and dig in.

The pitch is not the press release. While a press release needs to have some of the most intriguing information about the book, you, and what you are trying to tell your readers, a pitch is a "harder" sell. The idea is to consider to whom you are writing, and to reach out with just the right story at the right time. And, by the way, the first two or three sentences need to hook your target or it's all over. It's kind of like auditioning on Broadway. You have eight bars baby. That's it, so make them shine!

After you have grabbed the attention of the journalist, blogger, bookseller, or producer, you need to include what I call the "meat" or substance that your work will provide to a viewing audience. If your book has a strong nonfiction hook (recall I mentioned that your personal story can be the strongest hook, even for a novel), then you will need to explain the "story" that makes it interesting. If it is fiction, you will explain another story, except this one will be the essence of the plot or characters of the book. This is similar to what you have included on your press release, but not more than a brief paragraph or two.

The end of the pitch is anything else pertinent to the contact, whether it is an event you are doing in a specific market, or simply your (or your publicist's) contact information. Here are some sample opening lines of successful pitches for nonfiction and fiction titles.

Memoir/Business: Subject line:
She ran a billion-dollar business and changed fashion

Kym Gold, co-founder of True Religion Brand Jeans, changed the way we view and wear denim. This Malibu native is coming to New York in September to promote her book called *Gold Standard: How to Rock the World and Run an Empire*, in which she relates the story of her life growing up in California; being one of three triplet girls; marrying Mark Burnett and getting divorced; starting a t-shirt business on Venice beach; and years later, married again, running a billion-dollar company, and raising three kids.

Novel: Subject line:
NJ Family Therapist Dr. Laurie B. Levine pens
coming-of-age YA novel

How does an inappropriate student-teacher relationship form, and what are the lasting effects? When Maplewood resident and family therapist Dr. Laurie B. Levine heard that a female Maplewood teacher was arrested for abusive treatment of students, she pulled her young adult novel, on a similar subject, out of the drawer and finished it.

The two biggest mistakes I've seen in pitches are that they are too long in length, and not pointed or provocative enough. Clearly you don't want to create any "fake news" or overhype your pitch, which is just annoying to anyone reading it, but you do need to consider what will make it relevant. The pitch should light the fire and the press release, Q&A, bio, talking points, and everything else I mentioned are the fuel that will build the bonfire of interest from media and potential readers.

SECTION III

•

Reaching the Media

You have finally arrived at the action part of your campaign. Everything in the sections before is about planning and preparation, and all of this work you have done is as important as reaching out to media. Without a proper setup, you will be throwing pennies in the Atlantic with no one to see or hear them fall. I love the planning and preparation stage because at the end of it, you should be fully prepared to put together a media strategy with a full toolbox and a set of messages you feel best represent you, your book, and your brand.

The crash course in media that I am about to give will provide the knowledge you need to create your own media contact list, tell a compelling story, and pitch. You will learn that journalists, bloggers, and producers need to be approached and spoken to in different ways. I will give you an understanding of how bookstore events work and what other possibilities are available for public appearances. There is a lot of information coming, but I know with the organized planning you've accomplished so far, you are ready to take the plunge.

8.

Who are the Media?

Dictionary.com defines media as "the means of communication, as radio and television, newspapers, magazines, and the Internet, that reach or influence people widely."

I would agree with the definition with a caveat. "The Internet" part needs to be expanded because it is much more extensive than just one word. The Internet shares the same kinds of media outlets with the traditional world, which include traditional print-to-online sites, podcasts, radio, and video/TV, plus independent blogs and websites.

For the moment, you need to know the job titles associated with the people you can contact at the print outlets, blogs, websites, and print-to-online sites. The primary ones are: journalist, editor, critic, blogger, staff writer, assignment editor, and content manager. Under the editorial group there are many specializations, such as "Features," "Arts and Entertainment," "Calendar," and others that you can find by looking through the publication or site on your own, or checking out the masthead in different magazines. Broadcast has some of the same titles and some new ones.

When you are working on radio or television (and their cyber counterparts), you will reach out to producers, news directors, program directors, talent bookers, and story editors. There are additional job names you will encounter, but these are the main ones. Now I need to teach you how to communicate effectively with everyone.

Editors are often the people in charge of a section of a newspaper or online content. They may make the assignments to the journalists/writers/critics for stories that need to be covered. They may also have an editorial calendar with different topics that are covered at different times of the year. The most popular editor you will be in touch with is the book editor or book review editor. That person will decide whether or not the publication will review or feature your book.

If you have a story that is specific to a certain subject such as education or the environment, you can go to the editor who handles it. If you are interviewed or your book is mentioned it's what we call "off-the-book-page" coverage. Honestly, these days a lot of coverage is not in the book section because so many of them have been discontinued. When I started there was a separate book section at the *Washington Post, Los Angeles Times,* and the *New York Times*. Other papers had significant pages allocated for books. *USA Today* used to cover books and authors on Tuesdays and Thursdays, and they did some very big features. *People* magazine had a section called "Picks and Pans" and books could take up as many as four pages. Those days are over, and review coverage in a traditional venue is not that easy to get. Fortunately for all of us, the Internet has opened a vast world of book enthusiasts and opportunities for your book to be featured or reviewed.

Some people still refer to the Internet as the Wild West, where anything goes and the discoveries and treasures are available to the scrappiest adventurer. That's a fun way to think of it. After twenty-plus years of exploration, I will say that there are some rules and etiquette that you need to abide by to be taken seriously.

I come from the school of media relations that encourages communicating with the press that is most relevant to what I have to say. A woman's magazine, for example, is not likely to cover a book like *Iron John* or a diet book specific towards men. Sometimes you might squeak in for a Valentine's Day list of books to buy for your significant other, but it's a long shot. An environmental journalist won't be interested in a gourmet cookbook—maybe personally as a gift, but not as something to cover in the paper or online. This is why I suggest that you do a bit of research and become familiar with the outlet to which you are pitching and the nature of the contact's job. It will save you time in the future, I promise. For bloggers, this is even more important.

Bloggers warn us that if we present something to them that is inappropriate for their blog it could end up on the blog, but not in a good way. Bloggers are some of the busiest people you could ever meet. Most of the bloggers in the book world are doing it because they love books and reading. Many of them have full-time day jobs, and/or are mothers or dads. I'm not saying that you shouldn't be assertive in your pitching or that you need to downplay your work. I want you to be aware of the kinds of people with whom you are communicating. You also don't want to waste anyone's time by emailing someone who really isn't the right one for the job you need done. Bloggers recommend that you read their book submission or review policy page first, and then decide if and how you will approach them. When you are going after television or radio, the same rules apply.

Producers and talent bookers are common people to whom you pitch a segment/interview on television, whether it is for traditional TV or online video. The producer is going to be interested in the story behind what you are presenting, and the talent booker is going to be more concerned with the credibility and notoriety of the person (like you) who is going to be on air. I will get into stories more in another section, but in general, national television producers have a bit more time to plan. They will usually take your pitch to a meeting with the rest of the production team, the hosts, and the executive producer. At this meeting, they present your pitch just as you did at first to them, and the room decides whether or not to take it. There are layers to go through for these kinds of things, and you should also be prepared to have video tape of yourself readily available so they can see what you look like on television. Prior experience is almost always required for national TV like the *Today Show* or *Good Morning America*, although a hugely compelling story or news event could open a door for you, even as a novice.

Regional television is a bit different, in that these people are producing for local news and events. They are super busy, and when you approach them it usually needs to be in conjunction with an appearance you are making in the city or town. They rarely do anything by satellite unless it's a story that has already garnered national attention and is so relevant to the local audience that it must be covered in any way possible. You don't need prior television experience to appear on a regional show or station, but I recommend having some form of video of yourself available anyway, just in case.

National radio like NPR is similar to national television in that these producers have a bit more time to plan. Regional shows could get your pitch and immediately want to book you for the next day or the next month. It totally depends on what kind of space they have on a given program. In the case of radio, you also have additional contacts you can go to like news directors, program directors, and even the hosts—it depends on the station and the market. Some bigger cities like New York have strong local programming on their talk radio stations, but others around the country run syndicated programs to save money on production and personnel.

The big changes in broadcast have been a result of the corporate conglomeration of local stations. Clear Channel owns a large number of stations, and many of them pre-record DJs and play music selections organized by a computer. Some markets don't even have talk radio, and their news programs may be produced by one station and run on five or six others in the same city. If you subscribe to a database of media contacts, like I do, the same name can come up for a bunch of stations in the same market. All of them have different call letters, and yet they all fall under the same umbrella. Country, adult rock, soft rock—all may be run by the same company, with different music and DJs doing the voice tracking in an hour that is then blended into the music format for an entire show. I once worked with a writer on a book about the demise of local media and how potentially dangerous that could be. The story opened with a big storm out West that the radio stations were covering. Without their reporting and informing the public, there could have been many fatalities. With computers running the airwaves, that book is becoming more and more relevant.

The print and online local coverage that exists for many markets is a daily newspaper, a free weekly, and Internet sites. Pitching these places is a bit less formal, but you need to have a regional or community based tie-in in order to get covered.

Events are a topic we will get to, but for now I've given you a sense of who the media are. As you can see, it is a big group of contacts, and there is no way you will reach everyone. In fact, most people will not respond to you, whether you are a professional publicist or an individual author. Imagine the amount of emails and—in the old days—phone calls these people get? Look at your AOL or Yahoo account and see how much detritus is there and multiply that by a large number. We will talk more about the contacts and how to reach them. Right now, you need to understand more about stories.

9.

What is a Story?

It doesn't matter if you are a novelist, memoirist, or other non-fiction writer, poet, or cook: every writer thinks their story is one that needs to be heard by the masses. It's a prerequisite for writing, right? Why go through the laborious process of writing a book unless you think someone (or a lot of people) are going to read it? Well, it's time for a reality check. Ready?

There are billions of other people in the world, all with their own stories to tell.

Did I say that out loud? For our purposes, let's whittle the number down to something manageable because not every one of those folks is writing a book. I gave you a number earlier about the amount of books published in 2015, which was over 700,000. I think you get my point.

My job as a publicist is to evaluate your personal story and your book's story, and to advise you on how media-worthy those things are. With this book, I intend to impart the skills you need to do the same for yourself. How you shape your story is dictated by the nature of your work: fiction or nonfiction; prescriptive or memoir; mystery or romance.

For a novel, it'll be a bit easier to tell a story because you just wrote one! The level of audience interest is more of a factor of taste and is somewhat subjective. However, it always helps get a reviewer's attention if there is a story behind the story, or something about you, the events in the novel, and why you wrote it, that makes it more compelling.

We discussed this idea earlier when I asked you to think about why and for whom you wrote the book. When you are asking someone who has a full inbox or piles of envelopes full of review copies in her office to take the time to explore your work, every bit of information that can get you to that point is useful.

Case Study:
The True and Outstanding Adventures of the Hunt Sisters, by Elizabeth Robinson

The True and Outstanding Adventures of the Hunt Sisters is a novel, which is always difficult when trying to get booked on broadcast media, especially television. It was a story about a period of time in the lives of two sisters, one a Hollywood producer and filmmaker, and the other suffering from a terminal illness. It was based on real life events, which was key in getting media attention.

The process here was one of building blocks. First I pitched the national magazines and secured a solid amount of space for a featured review in *Time* magazine. I took this review, plus other book coverage in women's magazines, and brought it and Robinson's personal story to the *Today Show* on NBC. At the time, the *Today Show* was open to booking fiction, especially with a true life tie-in. They interviewed her for a segment on the show, and we used that appearance to kick off a ten-city book tour, which helped get the book on the *New York Times* Bestseller List.

For nonfiction, the narrative is either a personal story, as in the case of memoirs, or it is information that goes under the heading "news you can use." Here are some examples of stories that successfully got picked up by the media.

Case Study:
Diary of an Alcoholic Housewife, by Brenda Wilhelmson

Brenda Wilhelmson's book was about her experiences living in an upper-middle class suburb of Chicago with her husband and kids. She became an alcoholic and then had to face recovery in a neighborhood where "cocktail hour" was how wives blew off steam.

The *Today Show* picked up Brenda's story and sent a film crew to tape her at her house in Illinois. Then they had her on the show to do a live interview. Hers is an example of an inspirational personal story with an entertaining book about a tough subject. Brenda was also very good on television and had been on a local affiliate in Chicago for other writing that she had done in the past, which was useful in pitching her.

Case Study:
Vij's at Home, by Meeru Dhalwala and Vikram Vij

Vij's at Home is a great example of using prior media experience to get the producer's attention and book the segment.

Meera Dhalwala and her husband Vikram Vij run a successful restaurant in Vancouver, BC. On the Canadian West Coast their restaurant is very well known. In the United States there was virtually no audience whatsoever unless someone had traveled to Vancouver. However, Vij's Restaurant was a prominent spot during the 2010 Winter Olympics, which were hosted in Vancouver. NBC, which covers the Olympics, was there and taped a segment on the restaurant.

When the book came out in the United States in spring 2011, I was able to go to my contact at the *Today Show* to pitch Meera Dhalwala for a cooking segment. Fortunately for me Dhalwala and Vij are consummate pros and had made a good impression on the network. Combined with the cookbook, which was a take on Indian cooking that encouraged mealtime for families and recipes anyone could make, the pitch was a success and Meera came to New York to tape the show. The book sold over 6,000 copies in the US in the first several months, which is big for a title that was not originally published in the US, and was written by unknown chefs about a niche type of cooking.

Case Study:
Better, by Atul Gawande

Atul Gawande's book was about the global state of health care and how doctors and other medical professionals could do a "better" job of preventing and curing disease. There were different stories in the book that discussed the spread of germs in hospitals, as well as contagions in Third World countries.

Atul had prior media experience and a great platform as a *New Yorker* contributor. He did get on *Good Morning America*, but for his book we really needed a big print story to spur reviewers and serious book readers. I had pitched the features writer at the *New York Times* a story on the book and a chance to sit in on a procedure in an operating room with Atul Gawande. It was on the cover of the arts section with a picture of the surgeons at work.

The three cases above illustrate media opportunities for a memoir, a cookbook written by foreign authors, and a serious nonfiction book. There were different challenges for each of them to get a national booking. One common aspect to all of these campaigns is that the authors and I were able to present an idea that could work on television or in long format in print.

A story is unique in some way. It can be an incredible true life experience or a different way of presenting an idea that will resonate deeply for people. A very valuable story is one that no one knows except you. With something like this, you can have the upper hand with media and offer exclusives and other interesting ways of getting a big bang for your book at publication. For television, you have to be able to imagine your story in visual form and you also need to consider what the "takeaway" is.

Is there a moral to your story? Is it a product or service that is so incredible that you *have* to have it? Does it have interesting supporting characters and will people be inspired by it? Is it tips from an expert on something new and exciting in fashion, business, or health? Is it some kind of medical or spiritual breakthrough?

Journalists and producers are interested in stories. I either hear "What a great story" or "Where's the story?" We all want our stories to be original and wonderful, and they are for us personally, but media have a lot at stake, especially national outlets. They have to satisfy advertisers by having high viewer ratings, selling a lot of papers, or having a high quantity of unique visitors per month.

Watch television, read the outlets, and listen to the radio. This is the best way to learn what is in demand and how you might pitch your story. I have had people ask me to get them on *Oprah*, for example, who had never seen the show. Please watch the shows. Be an educated purveyor of media, and then you can start putting together your pitch and media plan. Later I will talk about how to create a story and other strategic tactics, but for now you need to build your media contacts.

10.

Building a List

So far we've discussed creating your personal contact list based on people you know or who might be connected to you through other people, social media, etc. It's time to venture into the unknown and create your media list.

If you have access to a media database like Cision, you can search for different contacts by location, subject, job title, and media format. Most regular people, not publicists, don't subscribe to this kind of database, which is fine because they are expensive. There are other ways to find out who to contact, and I'll let you in on a trade secret—publicists have to research contacts beyond the database as well, because many of the Internet people are not in Cision. Also, names change rather quickly in the media business, and you can't know for sure that the database has all of the current information.

Primarily you are going to research the Internet, and possibly use Lexis Nexus if your library has a subscription you can log into. Regardless of where you are getting your information, I am going to teach you how to structure your search so you know where to find the media outlets and contacts, you need for your campaign.

A novel, as I said previously, will get the most attention from book reviewers, book editors, and bloggers. If there are true elements to the book or your own story, you could get off-the-book page coverage. In addition, a self-published novel will get most of its coverage online, not from traditional print or print-online sources. *USA Today* and the *New York Times Book Review* do not review self-published books. You can always try, but as of this writing, these policies are in place. A traditionally published novel has more opportunities for regular print and online outlets. Even so, I would spend time researching online because the competition is still fierce for any amount of coverage in print.

For nonfiction, remember your story and whether you feel you have something strong enough for national or broadcast media. Online news sites, radio, and local media are all good. You will also be able to reach out to specialized and niche media depending on the subject(s) of your book.

Here is a step-by-step process for generating your own contact list using the Internet as a research tool:

1. Remember the exercise where we put down all the possible markets for your book? These "markets" can also be translated into media markets and individual professionals who cover these topics. I recommend you note them on a Post-it and put it right on your computer or desk.
2. Consider the books that inspired you to write yours. Are there topics in common? What are the books competing with yours? Write those titles and/or authors down on another Post-it and place it accordingly.

3. Open up a workbook in Excel or a table in Word (or hand write, depending on what you prefer). Set up your columns like this:

Outlet   Contact   Email   Phone   Media Type   Relevance

Outlet: The name or call letters of the media outlet, such as *WKRP, Good Morning America*, or *The Houston Chronicle*.

Contact: The name of the person or job title of person you are supposed to contact.

Email and Phone: You will likely only find an email address, but include the phone number if you find it for follow up. If there is also a mailing/station address listed, add that column to your list.

Media Type: National television, radio, Internet radio, a blog, etc.

Relevance: Is this a local venue? Is it your story that makes it relevant? Is it connected to your topic? List one main reason or word that reminds you of why you picked this particular media contact.

Put a header at the top of the page with the title of the book and the nature of this particular list. If it is a book reviewer list, put that. If you are including bloggers, add that title to the top. Basically, stay organized so you don't get overwhelmed.

4. Type one of the comparative titles you wrote down into Google search and see what comes up. If there are media out-

lets in the list of references to the book, click them individually and see who wrote the reviews, conducted the interviews, or runs the blog. Make sure to dig down through the layers of pages to get to the "contact us" page and find a way to reach a person, even if it's an online form. That's where your pitch will go if you cannot locate an email address. Now record all of the information you need in your document.

5. Once you've looked through three or four pages of the Google results, click the "News" tab to only get media stories. I like to look first at the results in general before I do this because I feel like some places get left off the news tab if they aren't "big enough." Repeat the same actions as I mentioned in Step 4.

6. After you've done all of this for your comparisons and competition, you can search by topic. For example, type in "health and wellness" into the search bar and see what comes up. Repeat the same process I mentioned for finding the right person to contact at the websites as you go through the search results.

7. If you are promoting a novel or serious nonfiction title you can search for the "top 100 book reviewers," "top 100 book blogs," "top 100 book review publications," or any other key words and phrases that pop into your head while you are doing this. I deal with the Internet in an intuitive fashion, so experimentation is my favorite method. You never know what you might find.

8. Take note of the "blog rolls," on the sites you visit, which is a list of other blogs and favorite websites that a blogger has,

usually placed on the side of a page. Usually a good blog or website will have other similarly ranked outlets on its blog roll. Make sure to check out some of those people as well.

9. Take your wish list of your dream media coverage, go to their websites, and look for information on writers, producers, and pitching guidelines. You can always email an editor and note that you are looking for the correct person to approach about a book. Many people, even busy media contacts, will help if you ask a sincere question in a polite tone.

Now take a look at your list and evaluate how you are going to proceed. Divide your contacts into people who will receive a copy of the book and those who will be cold pitched so that they may request a copy of the book. When I have a list of two hundred media contacts and a pile of seventy-five review copies, I have to be choosy when deciding which people to send copies to without first getting an affirmative request. For self-publishers, you will be paying for those books out-of-pocket and I imagine you will want to be as efficient as possible.

If you are sending copies of books to people, you will need to have their addresses. You can start another table or spreadsheet (in the same workbook if you are in Excel) to include just those people you are mailing to directly. That sheet will look like this:

Contact   Business/Outlet   Email/Phone   Address

Make a header on this form as you did on the first, indicating that these people are receiving copies mailed by you or your publisher, if you are working with one. I usually name the list "Review Copy Mailing." Using the same column headings (you can skip the address if you don't have it yet) create another page with just the contacts you are cold-pitching with their emails and phone numbers.

Finally create one last list with everyone on it that is set up like this:

Contact   Business/Outlet   Date   Action   Result

Whenever you do anything, whether it is a mailing, email, or phone call, make a note of what you did, when, and what happened. I also like to highlight individual contacts in green, indicating a booking or positive response; orange for a lead, but not a solid commitment; and red for an absolute "no." Continue to add dates, actions, and results as you go.

Other than analyzing your book and its subjects and creating a press kit and thinking about your pitch, list creation is one of the most time-consuming aspects of the work. If you like doing research, then you will be happy as a clam. If you find it tedious, then this may be tiresome and won't feel very inspiring. No matter what your personal reaction is to the work, it has to get done by you, someone in the publishing house, or an independently contracted public relations firm/freelance publicist. The good news is, once you have the list done and organized, you can start planning your media and pitch strategy.

11.

Planning Your Publicity Timeline

When to Publish

When you start a campaign and when you publish used to be very critical. It still is for some books, but not for all. Prior to the time of blockbuster publishing, books that were released were "launched." Publishers used to have nice parties, and reviews and press were timed to the book's arrival in stores.

Although the amount of books published has increased over time, the actual publishing of them has mellowed. Publishers don't have the money for big shindigs every month, and for some titles it is possible to get media attention beyond the first few months of publication. The basics of timing for publication can be determined with some parameters

Here's a trade secret: no one, not even the *big* publishers, know exactly when to publish a book. Yes, there are some givens, like making sure you are able to get into holiday and other specialty promotions like Christmas, Mother's Day, Father's Day, etc. Then there are books by authors that consumers are trained to buy in a certain month based on its availability. I'm talking about Michael Connelly, James Patterson, and others who write at least one book per year. Publishers also consider the competition for shelf space and marketing and publicity opportunities.

I should also mention the reason a book is usually published on a certain date is because of marketing and publicity reasons. We try to get books out there when they will be featured most prominently and when the media are interested in what the titles and authors have to say.

For self-published authors, I recommend publishing the book as soon as it is ready. I call this a "soft publication." Your "media date" or "hard publication" can be whenever you think the stars are going to align with media coverage and the success of your marketing—or when you think you can sell the most books!

I am going to break down what the norms are in terms of publication months, but first I need to address some lingo that is tossed around and needs to be clarified.

Publication: This means that your book is on the market and available for sale via any and all distribution channels.

Release: In traditional publishing this usually means the date that books are shipped from a distribution center to online and retail stores. However, I've seen it used interchangeably with "publication." I'm not saying you are wrong for using the word this way, but knowing that there are other meanings out there might help clear up some confusion.

Launch: This term is a pet peeve of mine, because using this word implies there is some kind of event attached to the publication of your book. If you are a celebrity or famous person and/or your book has breaking news that is going to dictate an entire news cycle, then perhaps "launch" is a good word to use. But I caution people about calling publication a launch, because I think there are inherent expectations associated with using the word that can potentially be cause for disappointment.

Having said all of this, here are some monthly breakdowns that I have generally experienced as the accepted publication patterns:

January (Or "New Year, New You")
Self-help; diet; inspirational; business: if you fit into this category, this is what the media are generally interested in around this period, and it's also what consumers are thinking about.

February
Self-help associated with relationships; debut authors; business; fiction: if you are a debut author, this month is not as full of new titles and there may be more promotion and media opportunities for you as a result.

March
Debut authors; mysteries; fiction

April
Women's fiction

May

Beach reads; women's fiction; biographies; books on mountain climbing

June

More beach reads; women's fiction; biographies or other nonfiction that will appeal to male readers on vacation or for Father's Day

July

Quieter month better for debut authors; more of what you saw in June

August

Debut authors; education-related titles; narrative nonfiction by lesser known writers

September

Public affairs and politics; serial authors in fiction and nonfiction; cooking; highly publicized titles by debut authors

October

More politics; cooking; big nonfiction titles by well-known personalities and writers; higher end photography books; art books

November

Photography; art; gift books; big names; and anything else you can think of that will sell in the current budget year

December

Good month for lesser known authors. A variety of books are published, including late-comers for Christmas or those titles that people want to get a jump on for January.

You may notice that the categories are not always dictated firmly in one month or another—this is what I mean about the secret. In the end, what everyone wants to do is get the book out there at the best possible moment. But you need to consider what you can control and what you can't. After you make your best educated decision, you have to go with it and plan as if it will be the biggest "launch" you've ever seen!

The Timeline

Let's say your official "media date" is March 1, 2018. Take out your calendar for 2017 and 2018 or print out calendar pages starting six months before March 1, 2018 (September 2017) and six months after (up to August 2018). Mark the big day in black with an "x" or whatever makes you happy.

In this model, your preparation for the publicity campaign should start on September 1st or thereabouts. Take out your marking pen and write "Go" or "Start" on that date. If you are traditionally published, ask your editor if you can connect with the publicist assigned to you and also find out if ARCs (advance reading copies) or galleys will be coming in, when, and how many. In your initial conversations with your publicist you will want to find out what the plan is for your book in terms of coverage and events/tour. If you want to talk to someone about digital marketing, you will probably need to find out who in that department will be your contact. In traditional houses, publicists don't handle all of the online outlets, but I can't tell you exactly how it's divided because it varies by publisher. In my shop, we do all of it because I consider online media to be necessary for a publicity campaign. I also know that coordination of the different forms, including social media, is a key part of a public relations strategy.

If you are self-publishing, you will want to determine how you will publish (either through a vendor or by setting up your own imprint). If you are thinking about hiring your own publicist, this would be the time to start researching and talking to people. Also see what kind of financing you will want to devote to the marketing and publicity of the book so you can decide if travel will be part of your campaign, or if you will handle everything from your desk at home. You will also need to make sure all manuscript files and book jacket can be sent in to your printing option of choice so that you will have copies available three months in advance of publication.

Do you remember all the preparation I talked about in the first section? Between three to six months of publication is when those things have to happen; the press kit, your contact lists, determining markets and audiences, and your press list need to be completed. Take out your calendar and make a note on December 1st, that says start pitching and review copy mailing. You will have gone through your list already, highlighting the people you want to receive copies directly and those you want to cold pitch who can request a copy if interested. All your personal notes to your own contacts should have been written and are ready to be clipped to a copy of the book and dropped in the mail.

The next date to be concerned with in this example is after the holiday period, and it may differ depending on where January 1st falls that year. I've found that emailing or phoning to follow up the day after New Year's is like barking at a wall. Nobody wants to be nagged about something when their desks are piled high with mail and other stuff that has accumulated over the holidays. I prefer to start following up late in the week if New Year's Day is a Sunday, or the following Monday afternoon if New Year's Day falls on any business day. Make a note on your calendar that says "Follow up" on the day you choose.

This is a general outline of what you need to think about when planning your campaign, and it is also an ideal model. All kinds of things happen that can throw off the schedule. What is important to remember is that the campaign starts before the book with proper preparation and set up. You want to be able to take advantage of every opportunity, so being organized and having access to all the information you need is going to give you an edge over the competition. Some other dates you can mark on the calendar are:

Events/Appearances: Record the dates for any readings or speaking engagements where you can promote/sell your book. Start as early as the six-month mark so you can have a postcard or business card made to pass out to audiences or potential contacts.

Pitching Magazines: A caveat to the pitching date I gave you is any glossy magazines you have on your list. In general, there is a four-month lead time for book coverage and even longer for features. You can try finding out on the websites what their requirements are, but in the absence of any information plan to approach editors four months ahead of your official publication/media date.

Pitching National Broadcast: Usually three months is enough time for most shows, but talk shows like *The Dr. Oz Show* or *Steve Harvey* could tape your segment and not air it for months. You don't have complete control over this, but I recommend you get in touch with these outlets as soon as your materials, like your press kit and review copies, are ready.

Pitching Radio: Radio tends to book between two to six weeks ahead of time, and then there are those stations that will ask you to be on tomorrow. I like to start my radio work about four to six weeks ahead of time and if I'm contacting the station too early, I make a note to follow up at a later date.

The months following your publication date are for building on the media you get, making appearances on outlets or events, and new pitches. In traditional publishing, you will find that their campaigns tend to end for most books six to eight weeks after publication. This is mainly because bookstores start returning unsold books as soon as eight to ten weeks after they hit their shelves. For you, the author, you can say your book is "just released" or "just published" for the six-month period I've outlined. My justification for this is that publishing seasons run in six-month cycles, give or take a month. It stands to reason that you could still promote through that season even if the books are only available in significant quantities online.

A side note: If you had your book published and feel that there were missed opportunities, you can either talk with a consultant about what else could be done, or you can pursue your own course of action. I have worked on a public relations campaign for clients whose books were published a year prior. In some cases, the campaign is also about brand management and awareness for the author himself, but I've also come on board to fill in the gaps that a publisher or an author on her own has not been able to fill.

Spread your calendars out on your kitchen island or desk and start noting the dates I've mentioned, as well as any of the other target times to accomplish certain tasks. When I first went to work in an adult trade house, Putnam, my director gave me the same advice on how to plan my season. In my case I had ten books and maybe five or six tours to manage over a six-month period. As I keep reiterating, the solution to confusion or chaos in campaigns is organization and details. Keeping a written calendar on paper or in Outlook that dings when you have a deadline is going to make your process a lot easier and more effective.

12.

Getting Reviewed

You have finally made it to the part of the job when you get to convince people to cover you and your book. This is where the rubber hits the road, and you find out how persuasive you can be—and how good a job you have done preparing a hit list.

I'll start out with a section of the media we haven't discussed much yet: the trades. Trade publications are important because they are often read by booksellers, librarians, some consumers, agents, international publishers, and film scouts. The main trades for adult books are *Publishers Weekly* (*PW*), *Kirkus, Booklist*, and *Library Journal* (*LJ*). For children's books, they include *Horn Book* and *School Library Journal* (*SLJ*) instead of the other *LJ*. Most of what these publications generally do is review books. Sometimes they send out calls for information for special sections and features for which books can be presented. Many of the rules for submissions are the same for everyone, but there are a few additional things you need to know about how self-published titles are considered.

One standard you can count on for all books is lead time. If you want your book reviewed in a timely fashion to coincide with a specific publication window, you will need to get review copies to the magazines in advance. For the most part, these publications have in-house editors who send the books out to freelance writers. The books are read and the reviews are submitted for publication. Once in a while, a member of the regular editorial staff will take on the responsibility for reviewing, but there are too many titles for a modest in-house staff to handle on their own.

Publishers Weekly is a weekly magazine with an active website. Its lead time is three to four months for reviews. It will take advanced reading copies or galleys, and possibly pages or an e-file, but I would double-check the guidelines when you submit. Policies can change regarding alternative forms of manuscripts, and it is always smart to check with the individual outlet for the current guidelines.

Publishers Weekly uses two different online databases to keep track of its traditional and self-published entries: GalleyTracker and BookLife. You or your publisher will need to register the book through the appropriate website. Self-published titles are sent through BookLife, while the traditional books are submitted via GalleyTracker. If you are going through the process on your own, you can look on the *Publishers Weekly* website for up-to-date information and instructions.

In addition to submitting the book for review consideration on BookLife, self-published authors can pay to be added to the listing in a special insert called "PW Select." This is a self-publishing feature published seven times a year in the magazine. Within the section are articles, reviews, and brief listings of what is available on this side of the market. We don't recommend that our clients pay for the listing because it's not a review, and your brief description is one of many. We don't think that there is much impact from it, but if you have the money and want to try it, it won't hurt.

I mentioned Richard van Anderson earlier and his book having received a "starred" review in *Publishers Weekly*. He was also named one of the rising stars in self-publishing that year. All of this brought attention for his book from a couple of people, who contacted him requesting information about foreign rights. He was even approached for a movie option. My point is that reviews in the magazine can have an impact if they are good, so you should at least register and send the book through BookLife three months in advance. Traditionally published books are usually submitted by your publisher within the same three-month lead time through GalleyTracker.

Kirkus, when I started, was a simple staple-bound, two-color monthly publication that contained all reviews and no other editorial content. It has since grown as a publication. Now it is a four-color magazine with features and reviews. Their website is also very active, and many of the reviews that don't get in to the print publication end up there.

Traditionally published books must be submitted three to four months in advance to the correct editor, fiction or nonfiction. Also, no matter how you are published, *Kirkus* will need two copies of the book, one for the editor and one for the reviewer (this also applies to *Publishers Weekly*).

There is a fee that Kirkus charges for reviewing a self-published or indie book. They promise an online review will be sent within six to nine weeks. If you approve of the review, they will post it on their website. Sometimes, they may print it in the "Kirkus Indie" section of the magazine. You can also pay a premium and get your review "express" so that you have it in four to six weeks.

I highly recommend paying for a *Kirkus* review. It is often read by movie scouts and other industry types that could bring you deal opportunities. Also, if the review is good, it is respected. *Kirkus* doesn't promise a good review and everyone knows that about them, so their endorsement of the book will be treated as genuine even though you paid for the reviewer's time in advance.

Another aspect about *Kirkus* for self-published titles is that it doesn't matter when you put the book up for sale. You can send it in for review at any time. You just need to be aware that it is better to have the review earlier rather than later so you can use it to build additional media attention. As soon as you are able to send copies of the book, I would get it done.

Library Journal and *Booklist* are primarily read by publishers and librarians. If you had even the briefest thought about librarians not being important, think again. They buy a lot of books, and that counts. The books may be free for members to read, but the libraries themselves have to stock them permanently on the shelves, without having the option of returning them. Bookstores will return stock, and the inventory that is sent back will not count toward sales.

Traditionally published authors can get into either publication the same way I've mentioned above. *Library Journal* launched a program for self-published e-books called SELF-e. There is a link on the resources page for more information. Generally, it is a platform for books to be submitted digitally and is curated by *Library*

Journal staff. If your book is selected, it will become a part of a digital lending system and potentially available to libraries all over the country.

Booklist says that they accept self-published titles, but because they are often unfamiliar with small publishers and indie authors, these books may not get reviewed. On their website, they recommend that you check out *BlueInk Review*, a fee-based review service that submits its "Best of" list to *Booklist* for publication every month. This is not a guarantee your book will end up in the publication, but it is a more likely route because *Booklist* is able to share the labor involved in screening and reviewing books with their partner.

Shelf Awareness is one of my favorites because I love the people who run it, and it was started as an alternative to other trade sources for booksellers. They are online only, and need the same kind of lead time so they feel they are getting a review out in time for publication. People who self-publish through their own independent press can get reviewed, but there isn't a way to ensure that it happens (such as the paid review for *Kirkus*). I would say that most reviews are traditionally published books, but you should always check the website to find out what your options might be at the time your book is ready. Remember, things change rapidly in the Internet age.

Reviews are opinions. Sometimes they are highly educated ones, sometimes they are more of a personal taste. At experienced levels of media management, a publicist might consider who is going to hate something before sending it, but it is extremely difficult to judge. One time I sent a book out to a bunch of bloggers in the

Midwest. The book was heavily set in New York City and had many references that were unfamiliar to non-New Yorkers. Needless to say, the reviews weren't terrible, but they weren't very positive either. Some people even said, "I guess if you live in New York, this will make sense." I learned my lesson there.

Another time when I was working for Bloomsbury Publishing, one of our authors received a horrible review in *Publishers Weekly*. It was ruthlessly negative and since it was his first novel, I was a bit surprised that they decided to print it. But they did, and the author was beyond upset. He circulated a letter asking for the name of the reviewer so he could confront the person directly. That wasn't a good move on his part because his actions were portrayed as threatening to the innocent reviewer and sour grapes because he couldn't take criticism. The moral of the story: please don't try to hunt down your reviewer if you don't like what is said. It is a risk to send the book out there, but you must swallow your pride and move on.

Publishers will send their review copies out to magazines, newspapers, and online sites within the appropriate lead time windows. I mentioned earlier three-to four months or longer for magazines and three months for the others. A publicist will include a letter and/or a press release depending on the department's policy. We used to send "galley letters" out with our advances, but later many people moved straight to sending out the press release. I recommend that you also send your Q&A, bio, praise sheet, and anything else you have put together for the press kit. The more information the better. Some people will discard the materials, but there will be times when someone notices a well-done press kit and you get a feature out of it, like I did once with *Elle* magazine. It was well worth the effort.

Self-published titles are a bit trickier because you don't usually generate advance review copies (ARCs) or galleys. These authors use their finished books as "review" copies and set a "hard launch" date to the book that is a target date for organization of media coverage and events. The hard launch is indicated on the press release and/or on a sticker affixed to the jacket of the book, so media people know that publicity is being scheduled for a date in the future when the book will be officially "launched." The other thing is you do not have the same opportunities for reviews as traditionally published titles because some publications won't take the book. It is so competitive out there and everyone needs to think creatively about how to get review coverage. When I want creative, I go to the Internet.

A traditional publisher might send out a hundred or more review copies to traditional publications. A self-published author will likely send only twenty-five and will save the other seventy-five for bloggers and websites. I know you highlighted your list with the books to be mailed directly and those to be cold pitched. Take out the cold-pitch list for reviewers and start reaching out to your list, one by one..

Do not send a pitch with a BCC to everyone because bloggers notice. I can tell when I'm on a bulk email, and I don't like it. It feels like you didn't take the time to personalize the message. We all know you are writing similar notes for all your contacts, but do send the emails one at a time.

Spend some time on the blog or website you are contacting,

and see if there is a way to tie-in what you are sending with what they are covering more directly. Then in your pitch you can say, "I noticed your article on . . ." or "I read your blog and know that you like cats, so . . ." Use the first two lines of your pitch to grab the attention of the person, whether it is something super exciting and amazing, or just something that you think the person will like. Tell him/her why you think so. People like to know they aren't talking to a wall online, so try to connect in a way that shows the person you care about what they are doing. Now the hard part: waiting for a response.

The rule in sales when cold-calling receives a positive return is twenty percent. If you write to ten people and get two people to respond to you, then you are doing well. You may get a quick response of "not interested," and you will also cheer when you see the words "sure, send me a copy of the book." Other common responses are "I'm busy right now, follow up in a couple of weeks," or "take me off your list." If you do this all the time, like I do, you will have a good idea of who will be responsive and who will not. If you are learning for the first time, you will need to be open to whatever the reply is, if you get one at all. The goal is to keep going even if you feel like you aren't getting anywhere. In reality, you have no idea of what is happening on the other end of your pitch, so try to be patient and tenacious about the process.

I've found that "fear" is the one thing that holds most people back from reaching out and from developing good pitches. Of course, you don't want to be insulting, and using the words "extraordinary" or "dynamic" just to create hype doesn't help either. If you are honest about your intentions and what you are looking for, you are more likely to get a response. It takes extra effort, but that is also how you will build a relationship with the contact that could benefit another book, or could enrich your experience in another way. If you don't ask, you don't get. I'm sure you know that expression. If you get a snappy response, chalk it up to a bad day. What is the worst that can happen?

On break from college one year, I sold merchant accounts for American Express door-to-door in Hell's Kitchen in New York, before it was gentrified. Was I a bit nervous when approaching local business owners about being able to accept "the card" with a fee that was more than what Visa or Mastercard charged? Yes, I was. I forced one foot in front of the other to each doorstep I had to get on, and went in and just talked to people. I don't remember anyone biting my head off in those early years of my work experience and I was super green.

To re-cap, for anyone seeking a review:

1. Send your best book copy, whether it be a galley or a finished print-on-demand title.
2. Include the press kit or, at the very least, a letter with the title so the person knows why you are sending it.
3. If you are reaching out online, personalize your notes as much as possible and don't spam everyone in a bulk email.
4. Pay attention to lead times and, if you are in the position of paying a fee, do it early enough to help build media attention.
5. Try not to take it personally no matter what type of response you get or if you receive a negative review.

13.

Off-the-Book-Page Coverage

Off-the-book-page coverage is what I strive for most of the time these days, especially when I'm pitching traditional print or print-to-online outlets. I mentioned earlier that book review sections have been cut or eliminated altogether, so finding alternative ways to get into the publication is part of the job. The difference between securing a review, a feature, or a spot as a source for an article, is the person you approach and how you position yourself.

The rarest story related to books in the mainstream media is an author profile or feature. There has to be an amazing hook about you and your life that will grab the attention of a features editor. Do you recall the story about Atul Gawande and the operating room? That's what I'm talking about. If you are going to pitch yourself for a profile, the person to go to is the lifestyle editor, arts and entertainment editor, or features editor at the respective publication. For online outlets add the web content editor or web producer to the list. If you have written about a specific topic, your options for contacts may be even more specific.

For anything related to health and wellness, you will want to reach out to the health editor; for science, the science editor; for gardening, the garden columnist, etc. Also, look for people listed as "writers" in the same subject areas, as they too may be potential interviewers and contacts. Your goal is to either have a story written about the book and your work or to be interviewed as a source for a story on a similar topic. Either way, you will get your name and your book in the paper or on the website.

If you need help figuring out what subject areas to research for the right contacts, go back to the charts you made about the potential audiences and markets for your book. That is where you brainstormed the relevant topics that could apply to your work. As I said earlier when I explained how to build a contact list, you will need to be very specific about your approach to these people. Familiarize yourself with other things they have written or stories that have appeared in their respective sections. Follow appropriate journalists on Twitter if you like, and keep track of what they are commenting on and writing about. If you aren't asked right away for an interview, it is possible you will be called upon in the future. If you leave the person with a complete sense of who you are and what you have to offer, you are more likely to be added to their Rolodex, cell phone, or resource list.

When you reach out to journalists, assume that there are a few questions you will need to answer in your pitch. If you aren't clear about what you have to offer, you will not get a response. The questions are:

1. Who are you and why should they listen to you? Include your credentials and expertise, endorsements, and previous media experience.
2. What are you offering them? Use your talking points and press release.
3. Why is your work relevant to what they cover? Add in talking points.

You see? The preparation you did at the beginning of this story will inform your pitches to journalists and editors.

Additionally, you should be prepared to answer questions about your topic and field that you may have or have not already addressed in your pitch. Depending on the person you are corresponding or speaking with, you may feel like you are being probed rather directly. If you get a person on the phone who has been writing for the *Washington Post* for twenty years, expect that you will have to be on your toes and sharp as a tack. Don't waver or stutter—as far as you are concerned, your pitch is the best one they will see/hear all day.

I used to dislike speaking to journalists for these reasons and more. They don't put up with hype, so don't even bother. You can expect that most of them have been around the block and if they aren't green, their editors are the gatekeepers that are more inclined to keep people out than let them in. Prepare, prepare, prepare, and then prepare some more. That is what I've learned, and now I have more fun pitching journalists than I ever thought I would.

14.

Getting on Television

I wish I could tell you that you could get on *Oprah*, but as I keep saying—no matter how many people ask me—Oprah does not have a talk show anymore. She now owns a network, called OWN, and it doesn't do too well in the ratings game. It seems to be a vehicle for her to do whatever she wants, whenever she wants. All the people my colleagues and I used to connect with at the talk show are no longer at their old phone numbers or emails. The best way to attract Oprah's attention is to be visible. The last person I worked with who caught her interest and ended up on an episode of *Super Soul Sunday* was Brené Brown. I will confess to you that it was not my personal doing. She was seen giving a TEDx talk by Oprah people, and that led to the booking almost two years after the fact.

Another super long shot talk show I want to get out of the way right now is *The Ellen DeGeneres Show*. I would not waste your time. For the most part, she books celebrities like Justin Bieber or Jennifer Lopez. Yes, I'm sure you have a connection somewhere who could talk to the person who cuts Ellen's grass, but I want you to watch the show for several months and then let me know how many general interest authors appear on her show. I am giving you the honest truth about these programs and people so that you can focus on the many other opportunities that truly exist.

Television is a visual medium and many times getting on air or not is a chicken and egg situation. If you had television experience, you could get an interview. But you are trying to get your first interview, so how do you do that? The keys are the story and the outlet you want to book. It is always a plus if you do in fact have prior experience and can provide a tape or file to prove it. However, you can get booked without it.

The people you talk to in TV are producers and talent bookers of varying levels, and the communication style when talking to these professionals is to be brief and to the point. Your talking points are going to be very helpful because most television interviews are between two- and four-minutes long. Questions and answers are spoken in "sound bites"—easily digested information that the audience can "take away" from the conversation.

Interviews that are one-on-one are often referred to as "talking heads," where there is one person asking the questions and one person answering. You are the "head" in this scenario. Other kinds of television appearances are guest panels and field pieces. A panel is the kind of set-up you see on *The Dr. Oz Show, Dr. Phil*, or *The McLaughlin Group* if you are a Sunday talk show watcher. A field piece is a longer format interview that tells a longer story. *CBS News Sunday Morning, Dateline*, and sometimes the cable networks do these segments. Usually the producers and camera operators go into the "field" with you to capture the sights and sounds that go along with what you are trying to say. Most of the interviews on television are "talking head" style, and I'm going to concentrate on them.

With short format media, grabbing the producer's attention in the first line or two of an email or phone conversation is crucial. Think of it this way: the same way you get a producer to take notice is the way your segment is supposed to grab the audience. We don't want people changing the channel because they are bored for a minute. These days attention spans can be so short, and viewers are ruthless with clicking the remote.

If you are sending an email, include your book title in the first few lines. (If you are on the phone, remember to verbalize your book title when you are discussing it.) Then write "In an interview I can address," and put your top five bullet points below. Add a line that says, "The press release is below for your review." End with your contact information and paste the press release after your signature.

Don't worry if you used some or all of your talking points from your press release in the pitch email. Most people won't read the press release at first, and it is more important for you to clearly express your contributions up front. If they are interested you will get a response and a request to send the book. Local television is easier than national, but you can assume that everyone will need to know what your strongest positions are regardless of how big the audience for the show or network is. Then if you are asked to be on the show, you have more work to do.

You've made it through the pitch and are scheduled for an interview that will either be "live" or "live to tape." "Live" means what you would expect: that you are being interviewed and transmitting in real time. If you are doing "live to tape," the interview will be recorded for replay at a later time. Most of the time, keeping the feel of the piece as live as possible is the goal so there are very few stops and starts. Someone in charge may stop the camera and will tell you where to pick it up again when things get rolling.

Here are a few tips that will help the television interview process go smoothly.

1. Ask your contact if they have a hair and makeup person or if you need to come "camera ready."
2. Ask when the call time is and, if it's a national show, if they will send transportation for you.
3. If you are recording the interview, ask before and/or after the interview when it will air.
4. Don't wear busy patterns, red, white, or plain black. White and black can wash you out, and patterns and red tend to "vibrate" under the lights.
5. Practice your sound bites or answers in front of a mirror, with a friend, or tape yourself in advance so you can be as prepared as possible.

I was asked to be on the *Today Show* as a self-publishing expert a couple of years ago. I had been interviewed on camera before, but never on live national television. I found the pace of that segment to be so fast, everything went out of my head except for the answers I had been coached to give. In the case of a big television interview, a producer walks you through the interview in advance, which helps a lot. I was grateful for the time we spent getting ready.

15.

On the Radio and Podcasts

Good news! The way you reach out to radio and podcasters is very similar to the way you contact producers and bloggers. The same rules for talking points, strength of your argument, and expertise apply, as do the recommendations for contacting online media contacts. Listen to the programs or podcasts first to get an idea of what the style of the shows is and whether or not your material will fit. Radio has many options, including national, regional, public, and commercial.

National Public Radio (NPR) is the most coveted network for authors trying to get media attention. In general, the top shows for selling books on NPR are *Fresh Air* and sometimes *The Diane Rehm Show*. Terry Gross, the host of *Fresh Air,* is a legend when it comes to broadcasting and interviewing people in the entertainment industry. She has an extensive following and many of them are book buyers. A case study I will bring up later is an example of how powerful *Fresh Air* can truly be.

Other important national shows include *Morning Edition, All Things Considered, On Point, On Being, Splendid Table, Here and Now, The Takeaway, This American Life* and *To the Best of Our Knowledge.* Many producers for these shows are based in

Washington, D.C., and they work for NPR directly. Some of the shows are independently produced and if you go on their websites, you will find transcripts and contact information to suggest a story or guest for the show.

Regional NPR stations are also very important in their respective markets for books. Some of the stations carry more weight than others, but that is usually just a factor of how big the media market is. For example, New York City is the number one media market in the country followed by Los Angeles at number two. New York and California are also often the largest markets for book sales. You can look for your local stations using the Internet.

Other book audiences can be found on Pacifica Radio Network, which is similar to NPR except that they don't have so much national programming. Their stations are found in individual markets. Also excellent are talk radio programs on FM and AM stations across the country. Some of these are set up for specific audiences and topics, so do your research. If you have a Christian audience there is an entire network of stations under the Christian Broadcasting Network umbrella (CBN).

Podcasts function more like blogs because they are run by a single person or a media entity, and they are based on the web. Places like *The New York Times* and NPR have their own podcasts, run by their own producers and hosts. You can look these up on the media organization's website. Other independent podcasts cover a wide range of interests, from fashion to food to healthy living to publishing. When you fine-tune your pitch for the topic you are proposing, look for the contact person or pitching guidelines on the website first and then go after an interview. I'm reminding you again to listen to the show before you pitch!

Now you have a very good idea of how to find the right media contacts, how to pitch them, and what to do in a big interview. All of what you have read so far is what I learned in my first year or so of doing the job. Combined, these make up the basic skill set of any publicist you meet. But if everything the job entailed was making lists and contacting people, it would be hard to justify an entire career or a publicist's ability to work with big names and celebrities. I'm about to open a door into my world that I hope will show you what a media strategy can do and how different strategies work. I'm not saying I can always make magic happen, but I've done my share. I have also been doing this long enough to know when there is potential and when there isn't.

SECTION IV

•

Advanced Media Strategies

16.

Creating Your Own Story

I am very excited to bring this section of the book to life for you. The knowledge you are going to gain will empower you as you work on your own, with a publisher, or if you hire someone. It will teach you to think bigger and may spark some wonderful ideas for your work right now!

Your book, you, and your brand are the three promotable entities in your world, so far. If the media aren't interested in what you are selling, then you are out of luck—or are you? What if there were other ways to make your own news opportunities?

Case Study:
A Voyage Long and Strange, by Tony Horowitz

Full disclosure here: Tony Horowitz was a known author when I pitched the idea I'm going to relate. However, he is the type of author who doesn't produce a book every year. He writes serious, narrative nonfiction, and *Voyage* was about pre-Mayflower American History. The book followed the trips and arrivals to the North American continent of various explorers, including Vasco de Gama and Ponce de Leon. There was a large opening section on Labrador,

Canada, and the people who settled there. Tony had done research in these places and for history buffs, the book was fascinating, but it needed to reach a broader, mainstream audience.

At the publishing house, we decided to send Tony on a book tour that would include some of the destinations found in the book. I took that map and the basis of the book to an editor at *USA Today,* and suggested the paper do a feature and then follow Tony's journey online and in print over the course of a couple of weeks. At that time, newspapers were looking for creative ways to link their print and online properties.

USA Today agreed to do the story and a photo shoot with Tony in Plymouth, Massachusetts. They put a map up online with red markers indicating Tony's stops. Tony blogged about his journey from the road and they ran excerpts from his blogs in the paper and continued them in full online.

In the Tony Horowitz example, the journey in the book to the ultimate settling of America was the "gimmick," and, along with the book tour, provided the opportunity for a media partner to come on board. Since Tony was a familiar name to many media contacts, he did get on regional NPR shows and his book was reviewed in the major papers, but the commercial audience was reached through *USA Today*'s generous coverage.

Currently I'm working on a project that involves a study and its results. There is no book at present, and the person who conducted the study is not a known entity. There are three media events that we have created that we will be able to promote through the media.

I put together a panel of academics with varying degrees of notoriety to be held at a well-known institution. The moderator is a host from a radio station in the area. This is a target event for media attention. We also have organized a community service project (target number two) that will take place over the course of a few months that can also be pitched to media. Finally, we are launching a visual Internet campaign based on the study's overall message. We intend to build an international community and approach online media partners to help spread the word. Since the study includes six countries in total, the global possibility is very realistic, and there you have target number three.

To develop ways you might create a media opportunity beyond your book, go back to why you wrote the book, what it is about, and the different markets that might like it. Look over your personal contact list and think about how far those connections can reach. I will go over events more in a later section, but you have the tools to come up with some ideas right now. They all may not work or be feasible, but writing them down is the first step.

17.

Breaking News

One of the most advanced forms of media relations other than creating your own story is to break news. Doing so with a book is very tricky because you need to do everything you can to protect the information before you are ready to go to press. At the same time, you need to be talking to journalists to get them interested so you can lay out a media plan that has the most effect at publication time.

Case Study:
An Unfinished Life, by Robert Dallek

Bob Dallek was one of my favorite authors to work with and his book had a lot going for it because a) Bob was a known historian, and b) the book was about John F. Kennedy and all things Kennedy sell. The editor had brokered a deal, without the publicity department's knowledge, with *The Atlantic* magazine for an exclusive excerpt six months ahead of the publication date. The excerpt detailed information about Kennedy's poor health that had never been reported. After my department recovered from the maelstrom of activity the article caused, I made a plan.

Fortunately, there was one more enticing tidbit of information in the book about Kennedy's relationship with a mystery mistress no one knew about, yet. I took the remaining information on his health, the mistress, and some other knowledge about Vietnam to NBC and got a deal for a *Dateline* exclusive and the *Today Show* appearance on publication date. The rest of the media had to sign an embargo or nondisclosure agreement before getting access to the manuscript so that I could protect NBC's right to first airing of the material.

Some publications won't sign embargo letters, and you have to take their word that they won't "jump" the date. *The New York Times* has done it several times. Sometimes it can work to your advantage for book sales because pre-orders can start building on Amazon and barnesandnoble.com, which creates its own kind of buzz. The goal of laying down a tight media schedule around a piece of breaking or exclusive news is to dominate the news cycle for as long as you can, create book buying interest, sell books, and hit the bestsellers lists the first week of sales.

An Unfinished Life debuted on the *New York Times* list at number one, and it is one of my proudest achievements. Bob Dallek hadn't ever been a big bestselling author and I had been able to "sell" a serious nonfiction book by an academic to a general audience.

Case Study:
The Good Nurse, by Charles Graeber

If you live in New Jersey you will know the story of Charles Cullen, the nurse who killed patients in hospitals across the state.

Graeber, a journalist, wrote to Cullen while he was in jail and Cullen agreed to meet with him. Over the course of many encounters, Charles Graeber learned the whole story of Cullen's life and what happened in those hospitals.

All this information was documented in Graeber's first book, *The Good Nurse,* and he and his representatives made a deal with *60 Minutes* for exclusive coverage of the story at publication. Here is another example of a media embargo based on information that was given to one source with a promise of first airing or release. But there was a wrinkle.

60 Minutes didn't have its piece ready when it was time to publish the book, and they couldn't guarantee an exact Sunday within a month of Sundays that the story would air. I was given the green light to approach a few choice outlets that were permitted, by *60 Minutes*, to air ahead of their story.

Remember what I said about *Fresh Air* and books? I wasn't kidding. Charles Graeber did one interview on *Fresh Air* and received an excellent review from Janet Maslin in the daily edition of *The New York Times* in the same week. In addition, the *New York Post* ran an excerpt that was about a different aspect of the story than what CBS was doing. The book hit *The New York Times* list that week with just three media hits. *60 Minutes* aired a couple of weeks later.

I relay these examples to you first, to show you that breaking news involves negotiating deals with the media and protecting their interests. If you have a story that you know is newsworthy and has not been reported prior to your telling it, then you can plan a strategy.

First you want to imagine your dream outlet. Where would you like to see your story told? Then ask yourself, is this the right outlet? Wendy Williams is great, but she probably wouldn't be the best source for a story on computer hacking. For something like that you would want to go to a hard news source like *The New York Times, 60 Minutes*, etc. If you have celebrity gossip, I would go Wendy all the way!

When you first approach a contact, you should send an email or call and say that you want to discuss an exclusive story. You will have to give a general idea of what your story is to see if there is interest from the contact. After that, if you are planning to send the manuscript, it is your prerogative whether you want to receive an emailed note with their promise not to release any information, or to get a signature on a more formal letter that you may need an attorney to review first.

Other kinds of breaking news stories and exclusives can include revolutionary health treatments; a miraculous event like climbing Mount Everest; or a first-hand account of volcano eruption that threatened a village. You don't necessarily need the next "identity of Deep Throat" story to launch an exclusive media campaign, but you do need something that is newsworthy for a general audience, or at least for a strong niche audience, like health and wellness. Watch, look, and listen to the media world operating around you all the time and pay attention to what is reported. If you do have a story that you believe is special, keep it close until the planets are aligned in your best interest so you can receive the maximum in benefits (and book sales).

18.

Inserting Yourself in the Story

To get yourself included in the reporting of a story, you need to be clear on what you and your book can contribute to the conversation. I am a big believer in entering whatever dialogue is happening at the current time. One of my goals as a publicist is to get my clients actively placed in the ongoing conversation, whether it is cultural, political, or educational. Now you know why creating those press materials and talking points is so helpful. With them, you can easily see what audiences you can reach and what pertinent information you can offer on the topics.

Initially you need to keep an eye on the news. The easiest way to do that is with Google Alerts. Set one up for all the different subject areas in which you are an expert. When the alerts come in daily (or more depending on your alert settings preference), check out the stories and see who is reporting on what. If a publication or online outlet has something for you, go to the article and identify who the reporter is. Usually you can click through to that person's email, or at least their social media accounts, and then try to connect.

When you do initiate a dialogue, make sure to explain what you saw that made you contact him, and why you are a good resource for the topic. The other thing you can do to become a part of a story is get in touch with the reporters who cover your field(s) in advance. You can send a note simply saying that you have credentials in these areas and would be happy to provide a quote or insight if they need a reputable source. Publicity departments and individual publicists do this all the time by sending out lists of experts they represent who can be available to the media when something happens.

The news cycle has sped up considerably as the Internet has grown, which makes jumping into an ongoing story challenging. Sometimes it happens on its own, which is a huge boon.

Case Study:
Men Against Women, by Laura McKinny

Men Against Women is a novel based on real-life research about the Los Angeles Police Department in the 1980s. Laura McKinny was working on the project for a documentary she hoped to release, and the precinct she was working with agreed to let her tape conversations. Before she could put her movie together, however, she was roped into one of the most famous murder trials of the twentieth century: the O.J. Simpson Case.

As it turned out, the tapes McKinny had were instrumental in discrediting Mark Fuhrman, a witness for the prosecution. Some people even say that the tapes were the reason O.J. was acquitted in 1995. Fast forward to 2015. Laura McKinny is one of our self-published clients with an important novel that is not about the case, but does have a basis in police corruption in a notorious department on the West Coast.

We tried the insertion techniques with her book during the difficult police shootings in Missouri and Baltimore, but to no avail. It seemed the media didn't need an activist filmmaker and novelist to provide her insight into a national crisis. Then we caught a break when Cuba Gooding Jr. starred in the TV series *The People v. O.J. Simpson: American Crime Story*.

Laura called up one day to let us know that she had spoken with the *Hollywood Reporter* because her character was going to be portrayed in the series, regarding the tapes. Here was an opportunity. A quick media list was assembled and emails about the show's airing were sent that afternoon resulting in interviews for *Vanity Fair*'s website and *Bustle* (a big women's interest site). The *Vanity Fair* interview was a huge coup and it was accomplished by swift action following a cracked window into the entertainment news cycle in a 24-hour period. We also received a call from TMZ, but in their case we had to decline. It was important to Laura to keep her story out of the tabloids and gossip sites. When you are a sought-after interview, you have the luxury of deciding what you do and don't want to do.

Proactive and reactive are the two words that best describe how you break into a story. To be proactive, you need to identify where or who will start the story; when you are reactive, you are jumping on something that is already spinning out in the zeitgeist. While it is preferable to get the phone call ahead of time, you can still participate in what is happening in real time. Be clear with your message, quick to respond or contact, and have the credibility to support your input.

19.

Building Momentum with Media

Media begets media. Does that sound like a cliché or a bumper sticker? Well it can definitely hold true in a number of ways. I mentioned the "building on media" concept when I spoke about reviews earlier. If you have written a novel or narrative nonfiction and you have received an excellent trade (or other) review, you can use the strongest quote from that review when you reach out to other media to get them interested. People like to know they are covering a book that has already been approved in the professional community.

Other ways to build is to target a big media hit at the outset that will introduce your book or story. An example is an op-ed in a big newspaper like *The Los Angeles Times* or *Washington Post*. Those pieces often resonate well with the NPR community of contacts. Other ideas are an interview on a national morning television program or nightly news cast. A local program can help you build in a region or your home town. Sometimes a significant quantity of hits can help you build up to a big target. If you have five women's magazines that have all reviewed your book, you can take those clips to television, radio, print or online media sources as part of your pitch.

All media hits will not be weighed equally, as you are now well aware. I could never put together an adequate list for you of what will or what will not produce another hit, but publicity is all about generating awareness. The more times you are able to let the world know you and your book exist, whether you are reaching a small or large audience, the more chances others will come to the party, too. Some of the work is trial and error and a big dose of common sense. If you are interviewed on an online program that has a listenership of 30,000, that's good for you. Will it get you an interview on *Morning Edition,* where millions are tuned in?

I have saved the most-debated building tool for last, the Internet. When I was working for publishing houses the mantra was the Internet did not sell books. That is not necessarily true, as I have seen online media coverage boost Amazon numbers. Everything doesn't do it, just like every TV program won't move the needle, but it does happen. The main use of the Internet is to create awareness.

If you watch the news these days, you will notice that many stories are pulled right offline. Whether it is a video gone viral or something funny on Facebook or Twitter, the net is a playground of information. The more traction your book or idea gets online, the more chances you can bring traditional media to the table. And don't forget that everyone is "googled." If you pitch your book to someone, that person will almost immediately type your name and the book's title into a search engine to see what's there. If there is nothing other than an Amazon link, you aren't going to appear very impressive. It doesn't mean you won't get anywhere, but it helps a whole lot if you have a presence online in the form of reviews, social media, interviews, or video.

My response to the people who said the Internet doesn't sell books has always been: the Internet sells people and ideas. If a concept, book, or product takes flight in cyberspace and your name is attached to it, you are golden. Building media attention with the Internet is a lot of work, but it can make a big difference. No matter how you call attention to yourself and your work, you need to understand that it is almost never just one thing that shoots you to stardom.

SECTION V

•

Events

20.

Bookstores, Libraries, and More

If there isn't a news story you can break or a news cycle you can hijack, events are another way to create opportunities for media coverage and book sales. Before I go into different kinds of events and how to set them up, I am going to give you a crash course in book distribution.

For all the authors or presses that wonder why their books aren't appearing in stores; aren't being sold in e-book form on barnesandnoble.com, but are on Amazon; aren't available for order if a store wants to get copies; and any other question that might arise regarding the overall concern of "why isn't my book selling?," the answer lies in distribution and sales. Just because a book is distributed, doesn't mean it is actually in a store.

In the late 1990s, there was a big "scandal" story in a trade publication about Random House not being able to meet demand because of a poor distribution channel. In publishing, we often call this area "supply chain." The reporting was very negative, implying that Random House might not be able to handle its own scale of production; couldn't get books to their warehouses; and were falling down on the job. There were reports of lost sales, angry stores, lost profits—a disaster as far as the industry was concerned. Today, with all the options for selling, the process is still the same in many ways, and vastly different in others.

There are more sales channels today than there were several years ago. Books are sold at stores, online, in digital form, and print-on-demand (POD). Indie authors may sell books through their own websites via an Amazon virtual warehouse process, while Amazon also sells the books on its site and sends them out through its own warehouse. Barnes & Noble has distribution centers (DCs) of its own around the country, so the books go from the printer to the publisher's warehouse to the DC to the individual stores, or directly from the printer to the Barnes & Noble DC, and so on.

Wholesale distributors like Ingram and Baker and Taylor also stock inventory, which is available to stores when needed. Publishers will ship from the printer to any stores directly when orders are placed prior to printing. Here's the thing: none of the places where books are sold will have the book on hand unless someone sells it to them. Traditional houses have a "sales force" and individual reps that handle Amazon and national chains like B&N and Books-A-Million, as well as people who specifically sell to Ingram, Baker and Taylor, Target, Walmart, Sam's Club, BJ's, you name it.

Here's another thing: if you think your book will appear at Barnes & Noble because you have a "distribution" agreement with your publishing agent, house, factory, broker, etc., you are misinformed. Distribution is about fulfilling an order, and in fact it would probably be better if it was explained as such when you sign up to publish your book on your own or with a publisher. If there is no dedicated sales team to sell the book "into" stores, it is up to you or your publisher to market to the trade and convince them to dedicate precious shelf space to your title.

If you are publishing on your own, you are either working through a publishing agent like CreateSpace or you are setting up your own account with IngramSpark. Both of these entities include "distribution" in their offerings and they will ship books on demand or when an order is placed. You can arrange to have Ingram list your book in its catalog with the thousands of others coming out at that time, but that is as far as it goes in terms of letting stores know your book exists.

Online distribution for Amazon/CreateSpace means that your book will be available on its international sites as well as ours in the US. This feature is included under their Expanded Distribution offering, which is a paid service. For e-books, it does not mean that your book will be available on barnesandnoble.com or Kobo. That is something you have to handle separately. Ingram does not do any digital distribution, and if you use a different self-publisher than CreateSpace, you will have to see what they offer to make sure you are getting what you want.

If you are being published by a small, independent press, the rules are very similar except that the press will set up the Ingram agreements, handle the paperwork, and take a cut of the profits of course. Another thing to note is Ingram will not list any indie book until it is submitted for printing, which is about three weeks ahead of a "pub date." So, if you do go to your local store to ask them to stock the book, they won't be able to order it until that time.

If you are published by an independent publisher that has an agreement with one of the big houses to distribute the books, or a deal with a company like Independent Publishers Group (IPG) or the National Book Network (NBN), there will be salespeople representing your book in the field. Just keep in mind that they have hundreds of other titles on their lists as well, so it is up to you, your marketing person, or publishing consultant to present the case that your work needs to get front and center attention.

There are many facets to these processes and how individual results will vary. It's a lot like publishing in general—very hard to figure out and difficult to predict. I am not saying that a book won't succeed because of a limited distribution. I am providing enough information so you can make decisions and ask the right questions without feeling like you are in the dark.

Case Study:
Love's Attraction, by David Cleveland

David Cleveland wrote his novel *Love's Attraction*, and started garnering attention from contacts he had in the film and television world. The hope was that a series would evolve from the story in the book. He self-published and spent a fortune on creating a beautiful, hardcover package, and hiring his own distributor for book stores. It wasn't that simple.

The distributor had no problem sending cartons of books to stores when they were ordered. The problem was the stores still needed to know about the book. It was set in Concord, New Hampshire, and had an underlying theme relating to Henry Thoreau—a potential local tie-in. We took a comprehensive list of bookstores from Rhode Island to Southern Maine and called them all to pitch the book for their shelves. David was willing to travel to many of them for signings, which helped. In the end, we convinced approximately half of the stores to stock at least one copy of the book. When he was scheduled to sign at the store, we were able to get a few more copies in, and David brought his own supply just in case.

BOOKSTORE EVENTS

The "author tour" started about twenty-five years ago in earnest when publishers found they could sell a lot of books quickly if their authors were visiting their fans in person. Some publishers set up ten, twenty, or more cities at a time and an author would go from place to place, just like a rock band. In order to maximize the benefit of having the writer in the city, there were a couple of different ways to make use of bookstores as event venues.

One way was to set up a "formal signing," which was a scheduled performance by the author in front of a seated/standing audience. Usually the format for this style of appearance was twenty minutes of talking or reading, a twenty-minute question-and-answer session with the audience, and a twenty-minute book signing. These times were all subject to a degree of flexibility depending on the author and the store.

Another option was to have the author appear for a "scheduled signing," which would entail sitting at a table in the store and simply signing copies for customers. When I worked with celebrities or big bestselling writers, we would set these up more often than the formal events. Having two hundred or more people in line for an autograph takes at least an hour, believe me.

The third addition to a tour was a "drive by" or "stock signing," when a publicist would call the stores in advance to find out a) if they had copies of the author's book in stock and b) if it was okay to come by to sign the books. You probably see books in Barnes & Noble and other stores that have stickers saying "Autographed Copy." They could be left over from a signing visit with an author.

Bookstore events need to be booked at least four months in advance for the big stores in the competitive markets. Politics and Prose in Washington, D.C., is the hottest independent store, and fall and spring dates are not easy to get. If you know you are going there, then call right away and speak with the events person. Smaller independents are less busy and can be booked in a shorter time window.

Barnes & Noble stores are contacted in one of two ways. You either need to arrange a visit with the corporate office, located in New York City, or you can reach out to the Community Relations Manager (CRM) in a local store. The bigger markets have the bigger stores that usually work with the corporate events people. You will know when you get in touch with the store how it needs to be done for that location. The same rules apply for lead time with Barnes & Noble. If you want to be seen at The Grove in Los Angeles, you will need many months of advance notice. If you are looking for the store in a suburb of Hartford, CT, you may be able to get in sooner. Your publicist at the publishing house will know how to arrange all of these things.

If you are self-published or published by a print-on-demand press, there is something else you need to know.

Bookstores are not always welcoming to the indie-published writer. I told you the CreateSpace story earlier, and I had no idea that there was such a boycott until I came face-to-face with it. If you have a publicist working with you, then she will be able to help you contact the stores and make arrangements. Most of the time the store will take your book on a consignment basis and you will have to fill out a form. Some stores charge an "event fee" for self-published authors, and there are those that won't host you if you aren't connected with a traditional house.

In support of the bookstores, I will say that they are within their rights to charge a fee for an event. Publishers pay "co-op" which supports the store having extra staff on hand, and advertising for the event in their newsletter and local paper. If you are asked to pay, ask the store what you get for the money. See if they will provide similar services to those I've described. Usually the cost is in the two-hundred-dollar range, which is what we were paying stores when I worked at Holt nearly ten years ago. Salaries and revenue just don't go up that much in the book business.

After you have scheduled your event at a store, mark the date on your master calendar. Now count six weeks back and put another note that says "pitch media for event in . . ." You can use the same process for your local contact list I outlined earlier. You can start pitching on that date to let the media know that you will be visiting. Include the location, date, and time in addition to what you will be doing—reading, talk, signing, etc. Plan to arrive at your event fifteen minutes prior to start time and don't forget to bring your pens!

Bookstore events have been popular because they are a way to generate media attention and reach out directly to consumers to make sales. More direct sales means less returns to the publishing house later. Also, many stores report their numbers to *The New York Times* and their local newspapers. If you have an author who sells one hundred books a day for seven days on a tour, those sales could be the tipping point that will get the book on the coveted best-sellers list. However, marketing budgets have been cut as have personnel in publishing houses so the author tour is not seen as the most efficient way to sell books. Added to this is the impression that there isn't as much media as there used to be, and other ways of making sales have to be considered.

Today, publishers and authors are reaching out to audiences through the Internet, and a new tactic for running up the numbers is to try to amass a good number of pre-sales for a book online. In this scenario, the awareness of the new book starts generating early so that by publication date, thousands of potential sales could already have been made. I am still of the opinion that events are important. I do agree that book sales may or may not be impressive at every one, but the media attention is worth the effort. What you need to do is look beyond the bookstores.

OFF-SITE EVENTS

What I like about events outside of a bookstore is the benefit of a "built-in" audience. Many places have opportunities for authors to speak about topics that are of direct interest to their communities. At bookstores, you are trying to attract a group of readers interested in your topic, whereas at other events you are providing a service by sharing your experience and expertise with a group that wants or needs the information. I will give you some examples of places to try and the best way to contact them.

LIBRARIES

A natural next stop in terms of places to get in front of an audience is a library. Libraries, even your local one, host author events. You can call your branch or, if it is a big venue, there is often an events or programming person who can help. Do try to set up any events in advance, especially at the large branches which may book six months or more ahead of time. When you arrange a date, ask the contact if it is okay for you to sell your book or if they work with a local bookseller. A publicist will know how to coordinate this arrangement if the library approves it.

CORPORATIONS AND BUSINESSES

Big companies often host authors as part of programs offered by Human Resources. They are sometimes called Lunch 'n Learn or Enrichment Activities. You can pitch yourself for one of these to talk about a wide range of topics from health and wellness to business. I've arranged talks for fiction writers too, especially in a genre like mystery or thriller. Remember to ask if you can sell your book.

ASSOCIATIONS

Groups like the Rotary Club, Chamber of Commerce, and the Junior League often host speakers or authors. You can go to their websites and search for different branches or chapters. Call the contact number or email the group to find out if they do these kinds of events.

CONFERENCES

There are a lot of writers' conferences as well as gatherings for every subject you can imagine. Search the web for those markets and audiences we identified at the beginning and include the word "conferences." Look on the site to find out if they are taking speakers or panelists. You can also get in contact to find out what their policies are and how you can apply. As with every other event, if you get to schedule a date ask how book sales are handled. At a writers' conference, it shouldn't be an issue, but no matter where you are appearing, you need to ask.

21.

Creating a News Worthy Event

The appearances I've talked about so far have a simple plan for reaching media. In all of these cases, your pitch is about an author event. Another way to build media interest is to design your own event.

The most newsworthy experience you are familiar with is the press conference or junket. Rarely does a book warrant an entire room full of reporters. If you have a celebrity-tell-all and the celebrity wants to use this kind of event to release the book, that's another story. Other popular media events are red carpet premiere's, awards shows (including the National Book Awards), trade shows, and festivals. For individual authors, the scale is not quite as large.

Some of the best ways to inspire the media to attend and cover your event are to bring attention to a cause or issue, to include recognizable names, to launch something completely new, or to pull off a stunt.

Causes

One of my previous clients was Hazelden Publishing, and they published a school curriculum on bullying prevention. There was a period of time when that topic was all over the national news and we took advantage of every opportunity. We also worked on arranging regional media coverage by setting up Bullying Prevention Summits. These were half- or full-day events that featured speakers and some break-out sessions. Parents, teachers, and community members were all invited to attend, and we would work on having a state or federal legislative official deliver the keynote. We didn't try to do these in giant media markets, but we worked on areas where they wanted to promote the program. The local television stations, newspapers, and radio would routinely cover the summits. If your topic relates to an issue of importance to the news media or something that is happening in your community, see if you can organize something around it. You don't need to have a full day extravaganza—you could even do a two-hour seminar at a library that features you and a couple of other experts or panelists.

Laura McKinny, an author I talked about in the media section, came up with a great idea. Since one of the reasons she wrote her book was to call attention to the problems with local police and community, she arranged a panel at an auditorium in a city near her hometown. The biggest paper in the city covered the event. The evening became a conversation between law enforcement and residents that illustrated some of the shared challenges they had.

Another writer I worked with had been a teenage model, and she wrote a short autobiographical story about her experience. A publisher affiliated with *The New Yorker* published it. Her plan was to call attention to the mistreatment of child models and her story was covered in some of the top online outlets like *Buzzfeed*. Then, we were able to upload her professionally video-recorded public service announcement to a major website that dealt with humanitarian issues, and she received a lot of viral attention. Even better, we were contacted by a New York State congresswoman's office about possible federal legislation that would put protections in place for child models.

Famous Names

Celebrity sells in this world, and if you want to ensure media participation in something you are organizing it helps to have some household names. When I say celebrity though, I don't mean you have to have Brad Pitt on deck. If you are putting together a panel of participants to discuss your book's topic, try to have an A-list expert in the group. If you are discussing politics, C-SPAN might show up to tape it. If it's an environmental issue, the local Associated Press reporter or someone who covers that beat may want to be there. I set up an event for Don Gross at the National Committee on US-China Relations, and he was interviewed by US-based reporters for Chinese television and print outlets. The media you need for your book and topic can be pitched for any event, but one with a credible source they recognize will help you get press.

Launching something new is like breaking news, which I've covered. The only note I have for you here is that new includes results from a study as well. Media love data and statistics, so if your work has previously unreported results and numbers, definitely pitch them.

Stunts

In the book world, I can't say I've seen many publicity stunts tried or orchestrated. But one definitely sticks out in my mind. Algonquin, a publisher in Chapel Hill, NC, once published a book called *An Arsonist's Guide to Writers' Homes in New England.* The "stunt" was to send a letter, authored by a fictitious writer, to book editors around the country in which they were asked to burn down Edith Wharton's home. It might be hard to believe, but some people took offense to this and the publisher issued an apology. They did get some press out of it at the time. There was news of the event in the trade press and a couple of other items here and there. It was original, to say the least.

Dressing up as gorillas and creepy clowns or coordinating flash mobs don't do the same things for books that they might do for movies. You still need people to open the book and read a page or two before you can really hook them. Media may buzz a bit, but the effort is not worth the results in this case. Brainstorm these ideas, sure, but make sure you don't get arrested or sued if you choose to try to make one happen.

Launch Parties

My final event offering is the launch party. I did say that publishers used to have quite a few of these and I've organized and attended some. They aren't done as often because they haven't been found to be highly effective for media attention or book sales. What I prefer to do is set up pre-publication lunches where the author is introduced to a table of media people interested in what he has to say. The key to either of these things is where you hold it.

If you want to entertain your friends, you probably don't need to go crazy on the place you have the party. If you want VIPs and media to show, you need to think about some place that will be of interest based on the food, location, and/or reputation. You know your city and where the cool places are. If you don't have a lot of impressive venues or media contacts where you live, don't worry about it. A party for friends and family that you can easily afford to throw is a nice gesture and a low-pressure way of celebrating.

SECTION V

•

Last Words

22.

Notes on Social Media

My company provides seminars on social media and I've found there is a wide range of knowledge and skill sets. Some people are versed well in one platform, while others are better at something else. However you slice it, social media is a part of a publicist's job because it can affect all of her other awareness-building efforts.

We do social media management because it's fun, and if someone is looking for overall brand management it's important. And as we know, the Internet can drive the news cycle and some online hits can sell books at Amazon and other e-retailers. For some people, social media can be overwhelming when it seems like every few months there is a new platform out there, and rumors fly about the demise of Twitter or the lack of interest in Facebook.

Over the past few years some of the dust has settled, and a select group of the many tools available for social media promotion have risen to the top as the best ones for people trying to promote books, ideas, and/or consumer brands. Facebook, Twitter, LinkedIn, Instagram, Pinterest, and Goodreads have all brought positive results to our clients, but how you use them and why is important. If you are an expert in a field, especially business, you will want to avail yourself of all that LinkedIn, Twitter, and Facebook have to offer. If you write fiction or literary memoir then Facebook, Twitter, and Goodreads are the best. If you are a designer, artist, or filmmaker, or have an idea or product that needs to visually present itself, you will need to use Facebook, Twitter, Pinterest, and Instagram.

There is so much to learn and because it is changing so fast, I recommend you take the plunge and start using it if you aren't already. If you absolutely hate the idea of it, then don't do it, because you won't be effective. Look into hiring someone to do it for you, or sit down with a person who knows how to use it and see if there might be a vehicle like Pinterest that might hold even a tiny bit of interest for you.

A tutorial on how to manage an effective social media campaign is an entire book, at least. For now, I say you dive in and go for the trial-and-error method. If you are just starting out you can't break anything, so don't worry about the results, for now. If you are interested, there is a basic social media guide that can be downloaded from our website. The URL is listed in the resources section.

23.

My Last Word

If I were going to provide one statement that sums up book publicity, it would be: "It takes a village." It is never just one thing that propels your book to a bestseller list or even to an impressive increase in sales. I started the book with the article I wrote for *Publishers Weekly* about what it is we book publicists do, and one of the bits they highlighted was something I said about everyone thinking that publicists are only good for getting people on those big television shows everyone assumes will be the key to success. They are not magic bullets.

It is possible to be on the *Today Show* and find that your sales did not jump at all. It could be the interview wasn't focused on what your book is really about, or it could be that the show was not the appropriate place to market your work. It happens all the time. We have learned that although one big hit is nice to have, it is more likely all of the smaller ones that are more tailored to specific audiences that do the job on a long-term basis.

Chris Anderson in his book *The Long Tail* discussed how it was the niche markets that were going to determine how the marketing industry was going to accomplish its goals. I have thought so much about that book as I've continued my journey in the world of media, books, and ideas. The Internet has made it possible to direct market to people who may be interested in what you have to say/sell. That is an incredible development. Where you used to need a newspaper, radio, or television hit to reach an audience, now you can "socialize" with a community of people that often come to you with defined interests and needs. It will take some digging on your part to find them, but given what you have already written, it is likely that you are already a part of at least one of your audiences, right now.

Will your research be as advanced as that of Disney or IBM? No, it will not. The point is you don't need to sift through millions or even thousands of data points to make a difference. You can hand sell your book to media and customers by identifying all the ways your book can speak to different audiences. Find the contacts that will provide you access to those markets, whether it's by review, interview, mention, or blog post. Then provide a compelling case for your work to be singled out for some attention. You wrote the book with a reason in mind, right? Share your passion with others. You are more involved with the topic of your book than anyone else and are therefore poised to take advantage of shifts in tastes, interests, and the market in general.

I know that my job is going to continue to change. For me, that is what makes it interesting. I enjoy puzzling out the problem of how to raise awareness of the property I am representing. I am always learning. And I teach people who work for me to be as curious and innovative as I think we all need to be. After having read this book, you have the knowledge to take charge of your own campaign, whether you hire someone, work with an in-house publicist, or do it on your own. This book is all about empowering you to make a difference. I know you can do it.

Resources

Case Study related websites:

http://rvananderson.com/

http://helenfisher.com/

http://www.donaldgross.net/the-china-fallacy/

http://gretchenarcher.com/

https://www.amazon.com/True-Outstanding-Adventures-
Hunt-Sisters/dp/0316159360

http://nymag.com/nymetro/news/people/columns/
intelligencer/newyorkminute/n_9781/

http://www.brendawilhelmson.com/

http://www.vijs.ca/vijs-cookbooks/

http://atulgawande.com/

https://en.wikipedia.org/wiki/Robert_Dallek

http://www.nytimes.com/2013/04/12/books/the-
good-nurse-by-charles-graeber.html

http://www.vanityfair.com/hollywood/2016/03/people-
v-oj-simpson-episode-9-fuhrman-tapes-laura-hart-
mckinny-interview

http://davidadamscleveland.com/

Books of interest:

The Long Tail: Why the Future of Business is Selling Less of More by Chris Anderson

Publishing 101: A First-Time Author's Guide to Getting Published, Marketing and Promoting Your Book, and Building a Successful Career by Jane Friedman

Successful Self-Publishing: How to Self-Publish and Market Your Book in eBook and Print by Joanna Penn

Your Notes

Your Notes

Your Notes

Your Notes

Your Notes

Your Notes

CPSIA information can be obtained
at www.ICGtesting.com
Printed in the USA
LVOW07s1235300717
543152LV00004B/523/P